ELIZABETHAN AND JACOBEAN DRAMA
1590-1640
in Context

Carol Leach

Nelson Thornes

Published in 2013 by:
Nelson Thornes Ltd
Delta Place
27 Bath Road
CHELTENHAM
GL53 7TH
United Kingdom

13 14 15 16 17 / 10 9 8 7 6 5 4 3 2 1

A catalogue record for this book is available from the British Library

ISBN 978 1 4085 1532 7

Artwork by David Russell Illustrations
Page make-up by Integra Software Services Pvt Ltd, India
Printed in China by 1010 Printing International Ltd

Acknowledgements
The author and the publisher would also like to thank the following for permission to reproduce material:

Images
p21 Duncan Walker/iStock; p23 Hulton Archive/Stringer/Getty; p31 Joseph Swain/The Bridgeman Art Library; p37 Sandro Vannini/Corbis; p38 Bettmann/Corbis; p43 Lew Long/Corbis; p47 (top left) Lebrecht Authors/Lebrecht; p47 (top right) Lebrecht Authors/Alamy; p47 (bottom) Lebrecht Music and Arts Photo Library/Alamy; p54 Pictorial Press/Alamy; pp 57, 59, 67, 68 (bottom), 69, 70, 72, 81 (top), 81 (bottom), © Photostage; p68 (top) Tristram Kenton/Lebrecht Music & Arts; p75 Universal Images Group/Getty; p79 (left) Hulton Archive/Getty; p79 (right) Kean Collection/Getty; p89 Bettmann/Corbis; p90 Luke Daniek/iStock; p92 Vetta Collection/iStock; p103 Fine Art Photographic Library/Corbis

Examination Questions
p6 AQA examination questions are reproduced by permission of the Assessment and Qualifications Alliance; p6 Reproduced with the permission of OCR; p6 Reproduced with the permission of WJEC.

Every effort has been made to trace the copyright holders but if any have been inadvertently overlooked the publisher will be pleased to make the necessary arrangements at the first opportunity.

Contents

1 Introduction

Chapter aims

In this chapter we will look at:

- the aims of this book
- how to understand Assessment Objectives (AOs)
- how to understand the context and backgrounds of the plays
- the importance of how the plays are received across time
- the importance of comparing and cross-referencing your texts.

Key terms

Context a range of factors affecting how texts are written, received and understood.

Genre a specific type of text. In literature there are three: drama, poetry and prose.

Period a particular time or era in history.

Contemporary something happening within its own time. This can be in the past or the present. For example, Jacobean contemporary matters are those happening in that period. Today's contemporary issues are those happening now, even at this moment.

Aims of this book

To the student

This book is designed to help you understand the context to this genre and period through the texts you are studying for A Level. It aims to help you be as successful as possible whichever examination board or course you are following. It will support you as a reader, a 'viewer' and a scholar of the key drama texts that we continue to study – not only because of what they tell us about the world and society they came from but, interestingly, about the one we live in now. **Read** the book, **use** the guidance and information, **undertake** the activities and **apply** these three stages – and of course **apply yourself** – to the texts you are studying and you will better understand how Elizabethan and Jacobean drama texts can be viewed as products of their contexts. It will also encourage you to consider how your own contexts affect your contemporary understanding and interpretation of these texts.

The book provides a key resource to use however it best suits you – within class work, group activities, revision and, significantly, your independent research and development.

Its purpose is to focus you on your A Level goals and enhance your study of Elizabethan and Jacobean Drama in Context 1590–1640.

One key to academic success at this level is the same as it has always been: an enquiring mind. You have to care. Not only about your A Level result but also about what you do to get it. You have to enquire actively into the texts of this genre, time and place.

To the teacher

Using this support material as part of your planning and delivery will provide you with illuminated contextual backgrounds and their textual applications that are accessible, time-saving, compact and relevant to your Scheme of Work and the teaching of the texts. You will have a key secondary source with pointers for further secondary sources to support your teaching of these texts in context.

Understanding Assessment Objectives (AOs)

At A Level English Literature, the Assessment Objectives are:

- AO1: Articulate creative, informed and relevant responses to literary texts, using appropriate terminology and concepts, and coherent, accurate written expression

- AO2: Demonstrate detailed critical understanding in analysing the ways in which structure, form and language shape meanings in literary texts

- AO3: Explore connections and comparisons between different literary texts, informed by interpretations of other readers

- AO4: Demonstrate understanding of the significance and influence of the contexts in which literary texts are written and received.

The primary focus for this book is AO4 and its application to the study and assessment of your texts.

It will also help you to get to grips with AO3.

How AOs work
The AOs are a guide to ensure that:

- you have consistent opportunities to develop the appropriate skills for A Level study in each lesson and study experience

- you have consistent opportunities to demonstrate the appropriate skills for A Level study in each essay you write

- the set examination questions always focus on the topic and skill areas that your course has outlined

- the coursework tasks designed by you and your teachers always focus on the topic and skill areas that your course has outlined.

Applying AOs to essay writing
AOs set out the ways in which you will be assessed in your examinations. They also help you to check that you are on the right track in your course of study. If you are being assessed in a particular AO you must demonstrate how you have developed that skill throughout your course of assessment as instructed in your examination board's specification.

So if you know that AO4 is worth half the marks in the essay you must write for a particular exam text or section or coursework task, your written demonstration of the importance and influence of contexts on that text is vital. You will need to:

- select the relevant contextual information that is demonstrated in your text

- embed the influence of contexts on your text, throughout your answer, in a clearly structured and substantial way. Even if the AO4 is only worth 10 per cent of the answer, you still need to do this but perhaps less substantially, so that you also focus on what else is being assessed (AO4)

- trace the keywords of the question from your introduction until your conclusion, linking the specifically identified contextual issue(s) to the relevant evidence in your text (AO1)

- prove how this context shows the reader something specific about the particular part of the text you are using (AO1)

- show that any comparisons you make with other texts are valid and support the relevant ideas in the question and your argument (AO3)

- show how your opinion, or your debate of the opinion of others, is relevant to the ideas in the question (AO3)

- organise your argument to show this to your reader – and only this, with no distracting or irrelevant contexts, text references, opinions and comparisons that take the focus away from what you want to say, in response to this particular task or question (all AOs, especially the skills of relevance and coherence, AO1).

Applying AOs to examination questions

A Level examination questions are always very specific in their wording and requirements from you. It is important that you take time to identify the keywords, how they signal which AOs are being assessed, plan and then structure an answer that responds **only** to the keywords. Here are examples of questions from A Level English Literature papers in 2011:

OCR

'The play's dramatic impact stems from deception and disguise.'

Evaluate this view by considering ways in which deception and disguise are used in *Twelfth Night*.

WJEC

'In his presentation of royalty in *Hamlet*, Shakespeare could be accused of undermining the political and social values of his time.'

Explore this view of *Hamlet* with comparative reference to Middleton's presentation of the ruling classes in *The Revenger's Tragedy*.

AQA B

Consider the significance of the supernatural elements in *The White Devil*.

Examiner's tip

'Stretch and Challenge'
Candidates who demonstrate how their studies 'Stretch and Challenge' them at A Level English Literature use the following 'high order' skills in their examination essays:

- contextualising relevant issues in the text (AO4)

- making meaningful cross-references that go beyond the immediate text (AO3)

- moving confidently between general and specific details (all AOs).

Activity 1

Linking AOs to questions and this book

1. Consider the examination questions above. Remind yourself of the title of this book.

2. Identify the keywords that outline the content of this book. Identify to which AO each one belongs.

3. Link each keyword/AO in the book title to the keywords in each question above.

For example, 2. '1590–1640'; AO4/contexts; 3. 'of his time' (WJEC)

Commentary on Activity 1

This brief mapping exercise will help you see how the book is relevant to your A Level study. It should also help you to think how to use this book to unpick the relationship between AOs and questions for maximum exam success. When you understand what is being assessed and how it is asked, you are halfway to applying the relevant skills appropriately in the time allocated.

Understanding context and background of the plays

In the next chapter, we will consider what types of context you need to understand and apply to your texts. First, it is useful to consider **why** you need to be able to do this.

Making context relevant

Let us consider something that affects us now in our current life in contemporary British society: think of your favourite music.

Maybe you thought of a song that you like. Now think about what you know about the singer or band. How did you find this out? If they are releasing music currently, you have probably heard or seen them in the mass media. You might know about:

- their style – how they look, dress, talk and pose. This could influence whether or how much they appeal to you.

- where they come from, how they live and what they stand for. Maybe you feel somehow connected with them or that you share something in common. Maybe you feel they 'speak to you' by representing your generation or social group and generating ideas that you are, or would like to be, a part of. Maybe you feel they have captured a moment for you or are reacting against one that you too react against.

If any of that is so, you might have chosen to find out more about the singer or band beyond what is obvious from a first look or listen. If you have, you are attaching importance to something about them that goes beyond the song in order to enhance your pleasure or knowledge of what you already like and know. You are linking the song to the circumstances in which it has been created and produced. You are seeking to put the song into context.

How we receive and compare

You might also want to contextualise the song because the singer or band is important or appealing to your contemporaries – your own friends and peers – and you want to be a knowledgeable part of this specific aspect of the culture that surrounds you: you want to engage the reception of the song. This might lead you to explore - **to cross-reference and compare** – through experience and research, other similar bands and singers to see what they are a part of and if you would like their contemporaries as well as liking them.

How context works

The contexts that you have explored might be about the **lives and behaviours** of the singer or band, their musical **genre and style**, their **musical and historical era**, their ideology, their **fame and popularity** at a particular time. This process is an ordinary, seamless part of life in our society – you do not need to study an A Level to appreciate the contexts in which your personally chosen music is conceived, created, produced, distributed and received.

Why it matters

Applying this process to any type of artistic product from any period in time may seem daunting, remote or even meaningless until you grasp why it matters: if you find out more about the factors that created the product then you are more likely to understand, and perhaps better enjoy and appreciate, the product itself and some others like it – or even different from it. This works just as well with products you dislike. Sometimes it justifies your dislike, sometimes it affects your initial opinion or reaction, and your reception of the product is modified as a result of your increased contextual knowledge and understanding.

Context at A Level

You are studying an A Level that incorporates the otherwise everyday activity of exploring the significance of context in your own life and times,

> **Key terms**
>
> Reception how we experience, understand and receive ideas, products and events.
>
> Ideology political, social and cultural beliefs and ideas.

as described above in the music example. A Level study incorporates an appreciation of factors of contextual significance for exactly the same reasons that you do with your music: Elizabethan and Jacobean drama (1590–1640) was not created in isolation, any more than your favourite music came to fruition in outer space. It is of its own time and world, inseparable from its contemporaries with which it will be musically or culturally interconnected. Your response to the music and the musicians, or to the drama and the dramatists, has as much to do with your time and world as it does with theirs.

To enhance our understanding of texts we can explore the following contexts as shown in the table.

Types of context	Focus
Historical, social, political, cultural	time, world/society and beliefs
Literary	styles and genres
Biographical	lives and circumstances
Reception	your reactions to these factors

Summary

This chapter has introduced the ways in which this book can help you to explore context as part of your study of any Elizabethan or Jacobean drama. You should now be more aware of:

- AOs and their significance
- the significance of studying a text in context
- how reception of text is part of context
- how comparison helps to put texts in context.

2   Types of context

Approaches to contexts
Layers of contexts
One context can sometimes appear more dominant or relevant in a particular play (or group of plays), but you can also consider how there are layers of context that influence the creation of the texts. The more you peel away the layers of context, the more you see what is at the heart of your text by observing how it has been shaped by its contextual influences. The significant types of context for you to explore are:

- historical and political
- social and cultural
- biographical
- literary
- reception of texts.

Macro and micro contexts
Moving in from the outside
One way to begin your investigation of these layers of context is by exploring the world outside of the play, the **macro** contexts and, working your way into the specific details of your text and writer, the **micro** contexts. For example, you could explore how:

- **historical and political** contexts influence every event and person in the period or 'times'
- **social and cultural** contexts influence some events and groups of people in the society
- **biographical** contexts concern the life and circumstances of an individual person
- **literary** contexts express the styles and concerns of the period, society or individual.

Text before context
Another way to approach context is to start with the text and your reception of the play itself, consider the literary, then the biographical and finally the social, cultural, political and historical contexts of the drama. This takes you from the detailed view, (the micro) to the 'big picture' overview (the macro). This way, you see how the text – what you receive or experience – can be traced to its roots on a sort of reverse production timeline, from today to the year and world in which it was first conceived. We describe this approach as **text before context**, even though they actually came into being the other way around.

Beginning with the text and working backwards is the most rewarding and useful way to study the drama and then write an essay for examination or coursework. Of course, you cannot put text before contexts, or take any useful approach, until you have a grasp of which contextual overview and details you must take into account in your study. That is how this book can help you.

Chapter aims
In this chapter we will look at:

- definitions of terms
- how all types of context work together
- how to approach the contexts in your text
- the importance of historical, political, social and cultural contexts.

Remember
Texts have plural contexts
All types of context work together to influence the creation of every text and its significance across time.

Key terms
Macro the overview or 'big picture': these contexts are concerned with the world outside of the play.

Micro the detailed view: these contexts arise from the literary and theatrical conventions within the text itself or from the individual circumstances of the writer.

Think about it
The context of reception
Response can – and does – change in any given place or time, influenced by the audience's own contexts, especially the 'receiver's' historical, political, social and cultural contexts. Have you ever changed your mind about something on a later reading or viewing? How had your own contexts changed in between?

To develop a contextual overview to support your textual study, let us consider what is so important about the macro contexts before we move on to the micro contexts in Chapter 3.

The macro contexts
Historical and political backgrounds
Developing an overview

Knowledge and understanding of the historical and political backgrounds of the Elizabethan and Jacobean period, 1590–1640, is key to a contextual appreciation of the plays you are studying. A brief and modest outline is sufficient, as provided in this book. To understand context at A Level, you will need to know what was going on during the period and how it might have been important to what you are studying now.

Once you understand that, you can develop and cross-refer your own ideas, weigh-up other ones (including those suggested in this book) and see which you accept and reject as ways into the plays. You will then be tackling AO3: interpretation and comparisons. You can also weigh-up how you understand and receive not only the plays themselves but even the contexts they appear to embody.

How can you begin to enquire into the contexts themselves?

Facts or opinions?

We may be tempted to consider all historical and political contextual details as facts and finite truth. However, when you start to enquire you will see how everything is subject to bias. As well as providing us with contexts (AO4), history and politics are all AO3: open to interpretation, comparison and connections.

Historical backgrounds

History is concerned with ordering and interpreting the large-scale events and movements that happen in any era.

Political backgrounds

Politics is concerned with who is in charge of history and society and why or how they are in charge. Politics is about power: who has and who has not got it, how it affects us and how we feel about that – as a society, or as individuals within the society. A political examination of history and society would start with a consideration of status, usually economic.

Generally, in any society, the people with the most money or material wealth, often linked to land and property ownership, are also the people with the most power. They influence and even control what we are allowed to receive as official records of the time, including literary records, not only at the time of production but across time to you: the 21st-century audience. Those in and with power are usually the ones to decide which versions of information on the big events (such as war, law, governance and dissent) will be prioritised and survive historically for us to receive in later times.

Gender, race and class

Issues of economic status, power and control are linked with social class, gender, sexuality and race. When you examine your text and observe how much it reveals about the world outside the play – how the English social class system operated and the ways in which gender, sexuality and race were viewed by the society at the time your play was written – you can see how everything you read and watch has political contexts. Your course of study and the examination itself are likely to reflect the issues of status, power and control as part of the importance of political contexts in your play.

Power, power, power…
You can enquire how:

- the playwrights who became famous and are since remembered or forgotten, studied or ignored

- the reasons the genre flourished or faded

- the content and the staging of the plays themselves

are all subject to the influence of who had power at the time each individual or group of dramatists was working on play scripts and theatre performances. Where the political power lies in a society is where the history is directed, even distorted, to represent what we remember and study. Rewarding talent and deciding who is the finest playwright artistically and theatrically is often, controversially, the least of a society's worries…

Historical and political contexts: in summary
As you can see, your grasp of the historical and political contexts will give you some overview to help you understand the plays you are studying. How you interpret their value can help you navigate ways into and out of the texts.

These macro contexts will be relevant to every context that you consider. And we do inevitably generalise – we talk and write about 'the Jacobeans', 'the Elizabethans', 'the 17th century' – otherwise, the detail becomes too fragmented for you to grasp the 'big idea' of this textbook and your study of drama in context.

Applying the context of period or movement in time to a dramatic text is a key way in which modern A Level Literature courses are constructed. This book reflects that approach, beginning with its title. Your activity in Chapter 1 has already shown that.

Social contexts
Social context usually refers to what we believe people were doing and thinking in any era: how society functioned and organised itself, and developed social trends and fashions to mirror its ideologies. Society – people in groups and as individuals – both creates and responds to the large-scale events and movements of the history that we receive and learn. Society creates, rejects or challenges the political systems we outlined previously.

Cultural contexts
Cultural contexts form a link between the macro contexts defined above and the micro contexts we consider in Chapter 3. Let us explore the meaning of culture.

Links

For more information, see Chapter 11, 'Theatres' (page 100) and Chapter 13, 'Chronology of events' (pages 107–108).

Think about it

Who has the power?
Investigate what happened to the genre after 1640. Why do you think this happens?

Link

For more information, see Chapter 4, 'The Renaissance context' (page 24).

Culture and literature

Culture embraces literary contexts, as it includes art movements and all art forms. For example, 'The Romantics' are a group of English poets with shared cultural ideas that included the development of their particular styles of poetry. What they believed in – their ideology – and their subject matter was reflected in their contemporary literature, paintings and music, in England and in Europe. This example of Romanticism, a cultural movement that includes literary contexts, shows you how the relationship between culture and literature can operate.

Culture and society

Most people live in a society but there are many groups in each society who consider their connections within their group (and therefore group membership) to be culturally based. People speak about 'cultural background', 'cultural events' and 'cultural interests' in very general ways. We often talk about belonging to a particular 'culture' or having a particular 'cultural background' when we mean being a member of a particular language, ethnic or religious group, or having a particular national and racial heritage, or to determine social class status or background.

Culture and the public

We talk about 'cultural events' when public social activities in the arts are taking place – such as new theatre, exhibitions of films and paintings, or live music, from subversive indie to mainstream pop to classical concerts. We sometimes link the idea of a 'cultural event' to national or ethnic groups if the event involves or concerns oppressed peoples. For example, across the world we have 'cultural events' for the Irish, Native Americans, Palestinians, Turkish and Iraqi Kurds, or Central American Mayans and so on to support and celebrate the ways in which these peoples and societies try to survive and to retain what makes them distinct from each other and the ruling nations or groups they struggle against. We use the term 'multicultural' to describe a society that comprises several of these different groups of people.

Using the word 'culture'
Culture and status

We talk about a 'culture dying out or disappearing' when a public activity, like Jacobean bear-baiting, or a language, such as Old English, no longer has anyone who practises or uses it. We use phrases like 'the death of culture' or 'the end of culture' or 'standards are dropping in our culture' when we feel that certain manners, genteel behaviours and customs and specific educational attitudes have become unfashionable or obsolete and no longer hold sway. We label people as 'being cultured' or as 'having no culture' when they are deemed to be either refined and sensitive or uncouth and unsophisticated. Here, the word 'culture' seems to be a synonym for a prejudice or value. We even have the phrase 'cultural values'; sometimes used to determine one's loyalty to one 'cultural group' or background.

Culture is everywhere

We refer to African culture, youth culture, football culture, working-class culture, aristocratic culture, mafia culture, the culture of the family, rural culture, the weekend culture – we even have yoghurt and bacteria culture. The most useful definition of 'culture' comes from this reference to yoghurt and bacterial cultures as it refers to something that happens in clusters and groups, in large numbers, with repeating patterns and formations.

The meaning of 'culture'

The only common factor in all these descriptions and definitions is that 'culture' includes the focused gathering of people into a range of social groups. For our purposes, defining (let alone applying) the term 'cultural backgrounds', and therefore 'cultural contexts', is often too broad to be useful.

Activity 1

Exploring the idea of cultural contexts

1. Which cultures and cultural groups do you consider that you belong to?

2. Which of your cultural contexts do you think would be evident to a reader or audience if you wrote and staged a play?

3. Could these cultural contexts also be classified as historical, political, social, literary or biographical contexts?

Examiner's tip

Selection of relevant context

Do write about the contexts identified in the keywords of the question and stay relevant throughout your answer.

Do not write about any of your wider contextual knowledge. If it has not been asked for in the question, it is irrelevant to your answer.

Cultural contexts: commentary on Activity 1

Much of what we define as 'cultural contexts' concerns political and social contexts or literary and theatrical contexts and reminds us how contexts are plural and interwoven. It is unlikely that you will consider 'cultural contexts' as a separate entity and more likely that they will be entwined with any or all of the macro contexts we have considered above and the micro contexts that we turn to in Chapter 3.

Activity 2

Revisiting examination questions

In Chapter 1, Activity 1, you linked AOs to the keywords of some examination questions and the title of this book.

Look again at the book title and those examination questions. Identify the types of context targeted in each question.

Summary

This chapter has introduced the types of context that help you explore any Elizabethan or Jacobean drama. You should now be able to:

• consider plural contexts

• see relationships between macro and micro contexts

• focus on text before context

• identify historical, political, social and cultural contexts and their significance.

3 Drama in context

Chapter aims

In this chapter we will examine the significance of the micro contexts:

- literary context
- how context is open to reception and interpretation
- biographical context.

Remember

Genre conventions of drama

A play is: narrative in action, structured into acts and scenes where actors enact the lines of the script.

Stage directions describe and guide the physical setting and staging, the appearance and behaviour of characters, background information for actors to realise the script.

Characters speak: dialogue (or conversation) with each other; a **monologue by** themselves; a **soliloquy** to the audience when alone on stage; an **aside** directly to the audience to hide something from other characters on stage.

See Chapter 9, 'Dramatic techniques' (page 80) for more information.

Key term

Revenge tragedy focuses on the motive, planning and execution of death by revenge – usually several deaths.

Literary contexts

Literary contexts are vital to your understanding of Elizabethan and Jacobean drama. They work in layers and contextualise what happens within:

- cultural and artistic movements
- the genre
- the subgenres.

Cultural and artistic movements

These reflect or challenge contemporary political and social positions. For example, Elizabethan England experienced the **Renaissance**, a significant cultural and artistic movement. The English Renaissance included literature; notably, Elizabethan and Jacobean drama. The word 'Renaissance' means 'rebirth'. It refers to the 14th- to 16th-century European movement that revived art and literature on ancient classical models. It spread west from Florence (Italy) to Elizabethan England.

The genre
Start with what you know

You already know how a play is different from a novel or a poem: drama is written to be performed. If you know something of how literary contexts operate within your text – the cultural and artistic movements, genre and subgenre – this should be your starting point for contextual exploration. Your investigation can lead to further exploration of the world in which the plays were written: the macro contexts of historical and political, social and cultural backgrounds.

The 'realisable' text

Drama is the 'realisable' text or genre. It is designed as a public experience and a group relationship between the:

- language and performance of the text
- actors themselves
- audience members
- audience and the actors.

Performance and delivery of texts change over time and across performances because of these public, group relationships. Your text is not a finished product. It is a script to instruct and guide the first receivers to finish it: the theatre company.

The subgenres
Dramatic variety

Conventions of drama provide literary contexts you can consider as part of your textual study. The drama genre, even between 1590–1640, has many subgenres, as we have in our contemporary drama. For example, revenge tragedy is an important and popular dramatic subgenre during the period. The many subgenres – different types of tragedy, comedy and history – make the drama genre varied. So the overall drama genre is **unified** through its genre conventions, as part of its literary contexts. It is then **varied** as a result of its subgenres and their own specific conventions, as part of a more detailed literary context.

Motifs in Elizabethan drama

Let us consider how a period, influenced by its macro contexts, produces specific dramatic subgenres as part of its literary contexts. We will examine how an Elizabethan play, *Doctor Faustus* by Christopher Marlowe, uses a convention of a dramatic subgenre: motifs. You do not need to know the play. We will apply the contexts to a typical example and you can find all you need to know in the information below. **Motifs** are symbols that represent human qualities and experiences. *Doctor Faustus* has motifs for the qualities of 'good' and 'evil', depicted as The Good Angel and The Evil Angel. This use of symbol is a dramatic feature of the period. It originates from an earlier period in the medieval morality plays that still influenced some Elizabethan and Renaissance drama. A moral figure appealed to the Elizabethan audiences and the motif was used in drama to guide characters how to behave.

The dramatic use of motif in *Doctor Faustus* reflected the growing Renaissance belief that people could shape their own destinies and decide between good and evil for themselves. The specific use of motif in Elizabethan drama is to advise or warn the characters, who can follow or ignore the morality figure in line with their own will.

This use of a motif is different from medieval morality plays which use the motif to pronounce and control the characters' destinies, either as a moral reward or punishment for their behaviour and sins on Earth. Here, the characters accept the moral and religious line and are saved. This medieval approach stems from their contemporary religious belief that fate was decided solely by the interventions of God and the Devil, where individuals had very little control over their own lives. This belief is linked to the Catholic ideology of Original Sin and the human need for supernatural help, or divine intervention, to stay on the righteous path.

Motifs and the Elizabethan audience

However, the Elizabethans still believed in Heaven and Hell as physical places and God and the Devil as physical beings that could be on Earth in person. The **social and cultural** context shows how a moral and spiritual guide is in the play to **direct the audience to judge the character**. The **literary** context – the dramatic subgenre of the morality play – shows how the motif **influences** the plot and behaviour of characters. The characters and the audience work together through the moral issues that the play dramatises. The **plot** of *Doctor Faustus* shows the presence and purpose of The Good Angel and The Evil Angel is to try to sway the character towards God and the Devil respectively. The use of motif shows the ways in which Faustus is torn in the play.

Motifs also function as a literary context as part of the dramatic **structure**. Their dramatic presence conveys the way Marlowe shifts between dramatic moods as Faustus's intentions shift. Dramatic tension is created when Faustus is repeatedly tempted by desire and power but plagued by feelings of guilt and repentance. An Elizabethan audience would have recognised the religious and moral dilemma of trying to resist temptation with its, to them, terrifying outcomes. Elizabethan attitudes towards dramatic morality

Think about it

Approval or challenge

Consider any Shakespeare play you know. How does the play appear to approve, accept or challenge the social and cultural contexts of which Shakespeare was a part? How does he use literary contexts of genre or subgenre to do that?

Examiner's tip

Learn the literary terms for the genre

Do make sure you understand the terms 'dramatic', 'realised', 'script' and use them correctly.

Do not refer to a play as 'a book' or use the technical genre term 'dramatic' in a lay-person's sense, rather than technically as a genre term.

Think about it

Appearing 'real'

In some plays, the story and characters appear as if they are real. Other plays have highly stylised rituals and conventions and appearing to be real is not the main focus. Both these styles are literary (dramatic) contexts. Some plays use both styles. Where have you come across either style?

Links

For more information see, Chapter 4, 'Contexts of revenge for the Elizabethans' (page 22), Chapter 5, 'Revenge tragedy' (page 38), a detailed guide to the subgenre and Chapter 12, 'Key influences on tragedy' (page 104).

Links

For more information, see Chapter 4, 'The Renaissance context': 'Shifting religious attitudes and beliefs' (page 25) and 'Ideas of humanism' (page 27).

Did you know?

Doctor Faustus

The play was first published in 1604: 11 years after Marlowe's death (at age 29), at least 12 years after it was first performed.

It was originally titled *The Tragicall History of the Life and Death of Doctor Faustus*.

There are two published versions, the 'A text' and the 'B text'.

It has provoked endless controversy and interpretations since its first airing, for all the above reasons.

figures stem from their social tension between the medieval ideology of the Divine Almighty and the new Age of Discovery.

Motifs and contexts in *Doctor Faustus*

Marlowe uses the motif in the dramatic structure to foreshadow the possible outcomes for Faustus. The angels indicate or predict what the Elizabethans believed would be the different outcomes beyond death in the after-life for a life lived in goodness or a life lived in evil. The **dramatic importance** of these motifs is of The Good Angel as a moral saviour and The Evil Angel as a moral corrupter. Their dramatic role (the literary context) is to help the audience choose the correct moral path for their own lives (the social and cultural contexts) as well as for the character of Faustus.

Applying context questions

The outcome for Faustus and the significance of Angels
Answer the following questions:

1. Faustus is constantly swayed by The Evil Angel and ignores The Good Angel. What do you think is his outcome in the plot?

2. Which Angel do you predict that Marlowe places last on stage in the dramatic structure, having the last word with Faustus and the audience?

3. Do you think this influences the moral message of the play?

4. Consider the contexts above. Who or what is really having the last word?

5. Use the information about motifs (for example, ghosts, devils, visions, religious figures) to consider how this convention and contemporary subgenre:

   - influences the plot and dramatic outcome of your own Elizabethan and Jacobean plays

   - is influenced by the social and cultural contexts of beliefs in this period.

Elizabethan motifs in performance
Consequently, there are two main ways to present the motif of Angels, or good and evil, in the play:

Dramatic presentations (AO2) Different interpretations (AO3)	Social and cultural contexts (religious beliefs) Literary context (subgenre) (AO4)
Played as characters on the 'Dramatis personae' list as realisable as any of the characters. They have both an earthly and divine role of moral guidance or corruption of tempted humans.	An Elizabethan macro context (based on older medieval beliefs) reflecting the ideas, genre conventions and sub-genres of the period in which the play was originally conceived, written and performed.
Played as extensions of Faustus himself – acting as his conscience. They are presented as the internal struggle to control your own actions and destiny based on personal moral choices. In films and cartoons they could be 'thought bubbles' or 'shoulder angels'; seen on stage as holograms, filmic visions or manifestations of Faustus's own imagination.	A new Renaissance idea (widespread by the 20th century), in which macro contexts show a world where Christianity is becoming an optional belief system not a social certainty. This responds to the modern subgenre of 'psychological drama' where characters are presented with a psychological profile and concepts of personal responsibility. Presented as an individual in a human crisis to whom the audience relates or not.

Motifs in your plays

You might have seen either way of performing motifs of Angels or other morality figures in Elizabethan and Jacobean drama. This example and exploration of a particular motif as a feature of a subgenre rooted in time is to help you to see a single text, for example *Doctor Faustus*, within a literary tradition and apply it to your own studies. You can now make comparisons between playwrights within the period. You can also contrast their contemporary presentations with those from a modern period, like the one suggested in the table above, influenced by different contexts of period and reception.

Open to reception and interpretation

Directors and actors interpret and emphasise (AO3) the same script in different ways and contrasting styles. This can happen with performances in the same period as well as interpretations changing over time because of the different contexts of reception and the receivers' (directors and actors) own social and political contexts. The variables of which words and actions are emphasised on stage, how they are said or presented and how they work for the audience provide endless interpretations and contexts of reception.

People can go and see the same plays repeatedly looking for new versions, interpretations and ways of performing the text to refresh the life of the script. This can be especially true if the play is hundreds of years old, whether popularly performed or seemingly forgotten. Actors can dramatise the same language, plot and characters but convey different moods and significances to their audience. A particular performance might illuminate something you missed on a previous occasion. Another might ruin the play for you.

Activity 1

Linking context (AO4) with interpretation (AO3)

1. Write a review of a drama production to which you had a strong reaction. Outline your response to, and reception of, the performance of the play: these are your contexts. Justify your response from the text and performance.

Here is a sample response to Activity 1.

An unfavourable review

A recent performance of *Romeo and Juliet* by a celebrated theatre company butchered the tragic mood so utterly by shouting every scene and line and storming and strutting about the place like Furies – as if the only emotions felt and expressed by any of characters was unbridled yet monotonous individual anger – that by the end, I could have murdered each one of them myself. I could not care less about the outcome for the plot or characters by then. It put my daughter off Shakespeare, put me off the theatre company and left us face-down in a box of Maltesers, in inappropriate states of disappointment and despair instead of the tragic catharsis I had hoped for.

Activity 1 (continued)

Exploring interpretation and the context of reception

2. Answer the following questions on the sample review.

   a) Consider how the reviewer's own contexts influence the interpretation of the performance.

   b) Identify the reviewer's understanding of the literary contexts in the performance.

   c) How do these literary contexts affect the reviewer's context of reception on this occasion?

Further reading

Reviews of your plays

Search online for recent reviews of performances of your plays.

Did you know?

'Tis Pity She's a Whore
The 2012 production attracted as much critical opinion for its whole-cast nightclub-dancing opening (AO3) as for the gore-fest ending – where Giovanni viscerally thrusts the bloody heart of his brutally murdered sister-lover (Annabella) at the audience (AO2). This variety of interpretation (AO3) shows the context of reception in action (AO4).

Remember

The world within the play is shaped and dramatised by the contemporary world outside of the play. Literature is not separate from the political and social contexts of its time.

Interpreting a play in performance

Modern versions of earlier drama, even when they perform the original text, can affect how you receive and understand the play, especially in performances of Shakespeare's plays. The current theatrical revival of Jacobean revenge tragedy explores how plays from the early 17th century speak to a 21st-century audience and how the dramatic features are used to make the play seem so current.

Sometimes a script is edited in ways the director feels will appeal to modern audiences and reflect his or her own interpretation of the play but people may disagree as reviews might show.

Interpretation, reception and you

We have considered how performances, versions and emphases change across place and time. The changes can often be traced to the political, social and cultural contexts influencing the performances at the time. The context of reception is also very influential. Who you are, why you are at the theatre, with whom, and so on, influences your experience of a performance of a play as much as how the theatre company interprets the scripts they receive and dramatise.

One factor to consider is that you might read your play before you see a performance. Obscure cultural references and difficult language affects your initial reception of a play from another period. As you study the play, familiarity affects your context of reception and understanding what the play has to say to you.

Debate about the influence of contexts on the text includes the playwrights themselves, whose individual backgrounds form the biographical contexts to the plays.

Biographical contexts

This is the most micro of contexts: what was happening in one person's life at the time of text production. However, the role of exceptional talent, extraordinary circumstances, chance and luck, can make biographical context appear more dominant than all the other contexts we have considered. When the dramatist is an innovator and has originality, their plays become the ones we study the most because they are the ground-breakers and blur the distinctions between genre, subgenre, language techniques and performance style. They invent, adapt and contradict their literary contexts, often importing and transforming a range of other (usually foreign) literary contexts. We study them because their individuality and complexity has fascinated and preoccupied or troubled us the most. This is reflected in how much critical debate (AO3) there has been on their life and work – their micro contexts – and their values and ideologies (AO4) – the macro contexts to which they responded. We compare them with each other, with their differently viewed contemporaries, their followers, their influences and even our own contemporary dramatists.

Who are they?

Elizabethan and Jacobean dramatists
The Elizabethans
- **William Shakespeare** (1564–1616): now the most revered and perhaps the most judicious in how he managed the social and political contexts of his time, keeping in favour with monarchs and powerful politicians. He wrote in all subgenres in both the Elizabethan and Jacobean eras.

- **Christopher Marlowe** (1564–1593): the most notorious and radical and no stranger to controversy and unconventional political and social ideas. He clashed with the authorities to his cost. He wrote Elizabethan tragedies and died aged 29 before the Jacobean era began.

- **Ben Jonson** (1572–1637): by far the most famous contemporary playwright writing in Elizabethan and Jacobean England (more famous at the time than Shakespeare). Very popular across all the social classes. He wrote comedies.

The Jacobeans
These younger or later contemporaries tend to highlight the significance of the three above. They form a 'second generation' of dramatists whom you might study from this period. Whilst they were all born in the Elizabethan era, the plays you study by them were written during the Jacobean era (in one case, even later). The depiction of extreme violence is often found in their plays.

- **John Webster** (1581–1627): repeatedly concerned with the inequality of marginalised social groups during his own time. He often challenged his contemporary political contexts of social class, gender and race.

- **Thomas Middleton** (1581–1627): collaborated with Shakespeare; for example, on *The Comedy of Errors*.

- **John Ford** (1586–1639): the latest playwright to be born. He wrote in the style of the Jacobeans after the Jacobean era had finished.

Elizabethan and Jacobean intertextuality
These six dramatists (and many more playwrights at the time) became mutually indebted and produced work that is intertextual. The dramatic relationship between the writers and their output means we consider them within the same dramatic and literary traditions as well as belonging to the same period.

The use of intertextuality highlights the Elizabethan and Jacobean attitudes towards the composition of a dramatic text. They did not believe that a

> **Key term**
>
> Intertextual has two meanings: 1 a text responds to ideas, language or direct references adopted or adapted from an earlier text. 2 within his or her own text, a writer refers to another's work or textual innovations.

Links

For more information, see Chapter 4, 'Contexts of revenge for the Elizabethans' (page 22), Chapter 12, 'Key influences on tragedy' (page 104) and Chapter 13, 'Chronology of events' (pages 107–108).

Examiner's tip

Regurgitating a writer's life story in its entirety in an exam will gain nothing – least of all marks. **Do not do it**, whatever the question. Only use **relevant** details, **in context**.

Think about it

Why have these plays lasted?

As you study the plays and read this book, consider what makes these plays popular today. Is it their social and cultural contexts and their depictions of humanity that we still find relevant and pertinent? Or is it the unproven personal life of the writer?

Summary

This chapter has introduced you to the ways in which drama can be studied in context. You can apply these ideas and frameworks to your study of any Elizabethan and Jacobean drama. You should now have more understanding of:

- the role of cultural and artistic movements
- the significance of genre
- the use of subgenres
- the importance of reception and interpretation
- biographical context.

playwright must create in isolation or even write down an authoritative script for publication. Scripts were not seen as books or literature during this period. Many Elizabethan plays were not even published until the Jacobean era and many Jacobean plays were not published for several years after their first performances. That is why we receive multiple versions of a single text: for example, Marlowe's A and B texts of *Doctor Faustus* and Shakespeare's Folio and Quarto editions – and why there are vague timespans of estimated composition dates for many plays by each of these dramatists.

Disputing or claiming authorship, or sole authorship, were not big concerns of the period. *The Revenger's Tragedy* has been attributed to both Middleton and Cyril Tourneur at different points in time. Middleton has now been chosen by many of our contemporary scholars as the likely author. They identified that the language use in *The Revenger's Tragedy* was more typical of Middleton's other plays than language use in known plays by Tourneur – but there is no definite proof. Middleton was also busy writing some of Shakespeare's scenes at the time, for which Shakespeare is now credited with sole authorship.

Thomas Kyd is a special case for you to explore. He was the earliest of these playwrights. Even though his plays are not much studied at A Level, he is acknowledged to be the forerunner of revenge tragedy written across this period. His play *The Spanish Tragedy* was hugely influential on Shakespeare and the Jacobeans. Marlowe lived with Kyd and was influenced by Kyd's use of dramatic verse. As an innovator, Kyd is included in this book for you to consider as part of the literary context and biographical influence that he had on the other playwrights. His play provides us with an insight into a key literary context that influenced Elizabethan and Jacobean tragedy.

Why is this section so short?

Gossip about the private lives of dramatists of any period won't help you to pass an exam, write an essay or understand text in context. In this period, it is even less useful as so little is known about their lives. The Intertextual and collaborative practices of many of the playwrights can make their biographical contexts irrelevant. The way that biographical context **can** be useful to your study of plays from this period is to:

- locate a dramatist specifically in time and place
- identify his contemporaries
- consider how his social class, domestic circumstances, education and travel experiences will reveal something about his dramatic choices of subject matter, language and setting – which we turn to next in Section B.

4 The world outside the play

Ruling English monarchs 1590–1640

During this period of 50 years, England had three royal rulers:

- Elizabeth I: the **Elizabethan era** 1558–1603
- James I of England: the **Jacobean era** 1603–1625
- Charles I: the **Caroline era** 1625–1642.

Elizabeth I: the Elizabethan era 1558–1603

The reign of Elizabeth I lasted 45 years but it is her final 13, beginning in 1590, which concerns your drama period. Many historians describe the Elizabethan era as the 'Golden Age' and the 'Age of Discovery'. It is famed as the time of the English Renaissance, outlined later in the chapter. The era embodied a sense of 'Englishness' that was marked and celebrated in three main ways:

- a renewed appreciation of classical ideals originating from Ancient Greece and Rome. The Elizabethan and Jacobean period is marked as a high point in English literature, especially in drama and poetry
- a thrusting colonial expansionism, through crown-sponsored explorers and raiders like Sir Francis Drake and Sir Walter Raleigh
- a powerful navy, whose greatest triumph was the defeat of the Spanish Armada and England's arch-enemy, Catholic Spain.

Economic and cultural prosperity

This was a time of increased national economic wealth and more power abroad. During this era, the arts 'blossomed', most famously Elizabethan theatre in the era of Shakespeare. In many plays from the period, the classical influences are clear, and we will look at some of these throughout Section B.

Some historians have presented the Elizabethan era as a time of general peace at home compared with the preceding years. By this time, Protestantism had become more accepted by a majority of the English people. English Catholic sympathisers saw the English navy crush Catholic Spain's hopes of invasion. However, it was also a period of considerable anxiety, particularly around issues of royal succession, treasonous plots and foreign wars. The notion of 'peace at home' is perhaps only in contrast with what followed: 17th-century battles between kings and emerging parliaments as the English people questioned the absolute rule of monarchy. Additionally, Elizabeth was the last monarch to rule England without also ruling Scotland.

Political and social strife

Strife was never far away, especially for the Catholics, including Elizabeth's cousin, Mary, Queen of Scots. She was executed to halt the political threat posed to the English queen. It was also a time of imprisonment and torture for dissenters and complainers, which might have forced people to keep quiet about their social and political grievances. The threat of the Tower of London is unlikely to have escaped people's minds. It was a time of plots, rebellions and attempted – failed – overthrows of the queen.

Chapter aims

In this chapter we will examine the world outside of the plays: the historical and political, social and cultural contexts of Elizabethan and Jacobean drama. We will focus on:

- ruling English monarchs 1590–1640
- Renaissance beliefs and ideas
- English playwrights and their plays
- applying contexts to text.

Queen Elizabeth I

Did you know?

The Age of Discovery
The English Renaissance is known as the 'Age of Discovery'. This thirst for new knowledge and methods of enquiry can be found in Elizabethan and Jacobean developments in law, science, religion, navigation and travel as well as drama and art movements.

Did you know?

Elizabethan dissenters

Thomas Kyd was arrested, imprisoned and tortured in May 1593 on a charge of atheism, based on a pamphlet found in his home. Sharing lodgings with Christopher Marlowe, Kyd tried in desperation to pass on the blame.

Marlowe was also arrested but later released – only to be killed in suspicious circumstances (some say by government spies) a week later.

Think about it

The Essex Rebellion of 1601

Supporters of the Earl of Essex financed a staging of Shakespeare's *Richard II*, at the Globe, to provoke an overthrow of the queen. They paid the theatre company, the Chamberlain's Men, so much money to put on the play it could almost be seen as a bribe to incite dissent. What does this political context tell you about the role and significance of the Elizabethan theatre?

Links

For more information, see Chapter 3, 'The subgenres': 'Dramatic variety' (page 14), Chapter 5, 'Revenge tragedy' (page 38) and Chapter 12, 'Key influences on tragedy' (page 104).

Remember

The Gunpowder Plot of 1605

This was the radical protest of English Catholics who felt increasingly disenfranchised under James I.

Contexts of revenge for the Elizabethans

Elizabeth I ran an efficient and centrally structured government, thanks to the English Reformation overseen by her father and grandfather, Henry VIII and Henry VII. This newer system proved problematic as many people resented the law being taken out of their hands to settle disputes, especially blood feuds of revenge. The problem arose when the law courts did not settle in favour of the plaintiff, appeared to act in self-interest or corruptly or did not even address the charges. The switch to Elizabethan, or Renaissance, values of a state-controlled justice system – from the previous feudal values of the Old Testament belief in 'an eye for an eye' – led to some indiscriminate and impassioned acts of vengeance, taken 'out of court'.

The Spanish Tragedy is notable as the first example of an Elizabethan play to address this tension in its plot, mood and tone, where characters take revenge as the state fails to dispense justice. The subject matter of Kyd's tragedy is the balance between injustice and vengeance.

The Spanish context

Despite beating the Armada, the powerful Spanish remained a thorn in Elizabeth I's side. England remained embattled with Spain in Europe over Portugal, experienced local trouble with Spanish support for Irish Catholicism and entered repeated fighting in the Americas over disputed territory in an Anglo-Spanish struggle for colonial supremacy abroad. Again, these conflicts are first highlighted in a dramatic sense by Kyd, in the plot and character relationships in *The Spanish Tragedy*. National and religious rivalries are at the heart of the murders in this play.

Activity 1

Acts of revenge
Consider the plays you are studying.

1. Where and how do the plot and themes depend on private acts of revenge where a state is perceived to fail?

2. How does the outcome and ending present the achievement of revenge?

All this aggravation was costly. By 1603 when Elizabeth died, the coffers were dwindling and power-struggles at home and abroad had become more pressing for the monarchy and the country.

James I of England: the Jacobean era 1603–1625

James I succeeded Elizabeth I (who had no direct heirs) in a haze over the legitimacy of his accession to the English throne. He was the closest royal relative of the queen but the law rendered him ineligible because he was not English. On the other hand: there was no other obvious candidate; Elizabeth I had not declared an heir in order to avoid further Catholic and Protestant splits; James I, as James VI of Scotland, had the advantage of knowing how to rule and be a king. The English aristocracy did not object; the English Catholics did not celebrate. Within two years, on 5 November, Guy Fawkes and his co-conspirators tried to blow him up. They failed and were punished for treason: hanged, drawn and quartered.

Public spectacle

Execution was a staged public event, like a piece of outdoor theatre for a live audience. It was preceded by something that resembled a **dumb show**, functioning in a similar way to a **comic subplot** or **comic relief**. Public execution was often brutal, bloody, ritualised and stylised. Sound familiar? Jacobean drama, from Shakespeare to Ford, exploits these dramatic features in the performance of its tragedies and acts of revenge. It seems as if art imitated life for the Jacobeans. Theatre was not an escape from reality – a play provided a presentation of reality. The dramas make us consider our emotional and moral responses to revenge and punishment, as part of the contexts of reception, in both the Elizabethan and Jacobean periods and our own contemporary society. The Jacobean reception of dramatic performances of revenge acts would also have been influenced by the public executions that they witnessed and the political and social contexts that these punishments embodied.

The public execution of Guy Fawkes and his co-conspirators

The king and politics

The reign of James I seems doomed. He began by inheriting an unmanageable debt from Elizabeth I and ended by presiding over an outbreak of economic depression and the bubonic plague. Despite uniting the Scottish and English crowns and nations and settling established colonies which founded North America and Canada, he could not secure his dynasty in England. Indications were that it would not go well for his son and heir, Charles I.

The king and the theatre

James I loved the theatre. During his reign, some of the genre's greatest plays were written. The king spared no expense in hosting and enjoying performances in luxurious styles and settings.

However, all this theatrical indulgence did not sit well with the public. In an economic depression, James I was seen to fritter the country's wealth on lavish, private entertainment. This would compare with our royal family or government, during this early 21st-century economic depression, diverting

Key terms

Dumb show short, often serious, ritualised episode without speech. A dumb show presents, mimics or foreshadows significant developments to plot or themes.

Comic subplot/comic relief comic scenes in tragedy that provide funny, light relief from the tragic plot and can emphasise important themes.

Think about it

Public executions and the theatre

Public executions are part of English history.

- How were Jacobean dramatists willing and able, despite royal patronage, to dramatise and perform acts of execution and revenge devoid of Christian mercy or morality?

- What does this suggest about the changing social attitudes towards monarchy?

- What does it tell us about the shifts in the political power of the monarchy during James I's rule?

Link

For more information, see Chapter 13, 'Chronology of events', the output of drama between 1603 and 1625 (page 108).

Key terms

Puritan a member of the movement (Puritanism) who believed in a basic, restrained lifestyle, both public and private, in terms of religious ceremony, entertainment, dress and behaviour.

Unsympathetic the reaction by the audience when they do not understand the motives and behaviour of a character.

Audience sympathy a response of care and understanding towards the dilemmas and fortunes of a character.

Patriarchy a political and social system of male inheritance and dominance, enshrined in law or/and culture across all social classes and family structures.

Did you know?

The name 'Malvolio' …
… is Italian for 'ill will'.

Remember

The Divine Rights of Kings
The belief that kings were put on Earth by God to rule the people and could not be removed by anyone except God – hence the severity of the crime and punishment of treason.

James I and Charles I were strong advocates of this belief.

public taxes and funds into exclusive celebrity events and personal luxuries. People might react. In James I's case, the Puritans, a strict branch of Protestants, did react.

You can see dramatic responses to the Puritan dislike of theatrical spectacle in plays like *Twelfth Night*. Here, as early as 1602, Shakespeare presents the comic example of a Puritan character in Malvolio. He appears ridiculous and trivialised and rather unsympathetic. Towards the end of the play, at his most humiliated, Malvolio attracts only a little audience sympathy. This presentation reflects the political and social context that the Puritan was the enemy of theatre as much as the enemy of James I.

Additionally, James I upset the new middle class, the merchants, who had some power in the Jacobean House of Commons. They supported the Puritan ideal of restraint and thrift as they saw the king channel their taxed wealth into royal extravagances. Disapproval from the merchant class further narrowed James I's support-base. These social and political tensions would soon come to a head with Charles I.

Charles I: the Caroline era 1625–1642
Monarchy in crisis
Charles I is remembered for the English Civil Wars between 1642 and 1651 and for losing the throne to Parliament by 1649. The era of absolute rule by the monarchy was over. The earlier belief in The Divine Right of Kings (kings as monarchs were primarily male within patriarchy) had been severely challenged. By 1649, Charles I was dead, executed by the new Commonwealth rulers of England. How had this happened? Charles I had alienated his people: he married a Catholic princess, sought to unite Ireland with England and Scotland and dissolved parliament early in his reign. These actions caused the population to worry that England was returning to the pre-Reformation days of an absolute rule, which they had not experienced under Elizabeth I and James I. The fear of absolutism was instrumental in the support for parliamentary reform, the Puritans, the Commonwealth and the end – albeit temporarily – of the monarchy during this period.

Theatre in crisis
The power of the Puritans under Oliver Cromwell grew. Once in power, they closed the theatres in 1642. That was the end of Jacobean drama; of any English drama, until 1660 and the Restoration of the Monarchy when Charles II came to the throne. The genre had already dwindled by the end of the 1620s as Charles I was far too distracted by his conflicts with Parliament to promote enjoyment of the theatre. The great dramatists of the Elizabethan and Jacobean eras were either dead or no longer writing plays of significance by 1625. The exception is John Ford, whose play *'Tis Pity She's a Whore* was written somewhere between 1629 and 1633.

The Renaissance context
The Elizabethan era is generally regarded as the height of the English Renaissance. It is a cultural phenomenon spanning a range of important developments with plural contexts. Earlier in the chapter, you read an outline of some defining features of the Renaissance. The English Renaissance can be explored through some of the Elizabethan, and the

Jacobean, society's key beliefs, attitudes and understanding of the world around them. Let us consider these important aspects of the Renaissance:

- shifting religious beliefs and attitudes
- influence of classical ideals
- ideas of humanism
- the notion of 'Renaissance Man'
- interest in foreign travel
- the widespread English theatre scene.

Shifting religious attitudes and beliefs

The transition to Protestantism

Elizabethan England rejected the Catholic religion and became a Protestant country. You know that despite this official line some Jacobeans remained unhappy with that shift, expressed in the Gunpowder Plot of 1605. You also know how the Puritans responded to Charles I's attempts at a greater union with Catholic countries and beliefs as a result of his Catholic marriage. You can see how tensions might develop between the expression of old beliefs and superstitions and these inconsistent state-driven demands for religious reform. It is likely that Elizabethan and Jacobean society would have embraced some contradictory religious attitudes as a result. Controversial social issues would include the following.

1. A suspicion of spirits from the after-life, such as ghosts, visions and supernatural bodies. The Protestant faith rejected the Catholic notion of Purgatory, a sort of waiting room between Heaven and Hell, where unresolved souls were suspended as they awaited judgement on their divine fate. Ghosts were then viewed as devilish and deceptive, not to be trusted by a Protestant Christian on earth. However, there was still a Jacobean belief in magic and witches. Remember *Macbeth* was written in 1605–1606.

2. A suspicion of all things Italian, from the Pope – as head of the Catholic Church and faith – to politics, which Protestants deemed corrupt, lascivious and Machiavellian in nature – a real clash with the Humanist ideals of the English Renaissance.

The King James Bible

In 1604, the year after he became King of England, James I ordered the translation of the Bible from the Hebrew, Greek and Latin into English. In 1611 the King James version of the Holy Bible was issued. It was widely used as the definitive English version until well into the 18th century. It is still available today, known as 'The Authorised Version'.

James I instructed his translators – 47 Protestant scholars – that his version must reflect the theological beliefs and organisation of the Church of England, especially the Church's ideology on the ordinance into Holy Orders. This move signified that there would be no return to Catholicism as the dominant religion or the Pope as the head of the Church.

The King James Bible was not only a translation, it was a message that Protestantism was now **the** English and Scottish religion – and that message

Did you know?

The Great Chain of Being
This is the Elizabethan belief in an ordered hierarchy of divine importance (and therefore of social and political position and power). God is at the top, the lowliest animals are at the bottom. Underneath God and the angels is the King followed by human beings in the order of their social class. This belief supports the idea of the Divine Right of Kings, as they were next to God in importance. The lower your social status, the further down you were.

Think about it

Ghosts, Italians and Catholics
Consider the presentations of these three character types in your plays. Consider if you, or the audience, is encouraged – or even directed – to trust or sympathise with their characters or manifestations in the play.

Did you know?

Italian settings were very popular in Elizabethan and Jacobean drama. See if and how 'the Italian world' is used in your own plays.

Links

For more information, see Chapter 8, 'Significant character types': 'Church officials and religious figures' (page 69) and Chapter 10, 'The dramatic significance of Italy' (page 90).

was controlled through the theological literature. For many Jacobeans, this might be the only book they read or heard aloud in church. This Bible had an influence on wider literature. Once the Bible was available, it became the source of biblical references which have appeared in English literature ever since.

The influence of classical ideals

Shifting religious ideologies during the Renaissance included an interest in pre-Christian cultures of Ancient Greece and Rome. You are likely to observe the influence of classical ideals as part of the cultural and literary contexts in your plays. The celebration and revival of Greek and Roman knowledge, culture and literature in your play can be contextualised in the following ways.

Non-Christian gods

References are to a mythical world ruled by pre-Christian gods and deities, pagan or Ancient Greek and Roman. Such references might appear to provide a religious context but, as figures from Greek or Roman mythology, the pre-Christian references are examples of how shifting religious attitudes during the Renaissance paved the way for Humanist beliefs.

Language

The classical references often function as metaphors that symbolise a comparison between the human qualities demonstrated by characters in your play and the mythical qualities traditionally associated with the classical figures identified in the reference. These are called **allusions**. Sometimes the allusion refers directly to the myth or character; at other times it is implied through reference to key elements of the myth. In your play/s, identify whether the classical references to myth and language are made directly or indirectly. Consider its effect on the description or comparison of a character in your play.

The reference might elevate and dignify your character in the context of this cultural aspiration to the classical ideal or it could warn the audience of the character's fate if their classical role-model met a sticky end. The *Doctor Faustus* extract, later in this chapter, features examples of both of these outcomes.

The language in your play might include Latin or Ancient Greek vocabulary, phrases and mottos, alongside or interwoven with the English. Use of a classical language in the play demonstrates the classical education of the dramatist and would have been familiar to the educated classes and scholars in the audience.

Your play could also refer to an aspect of classical knowledge from the spheres of astronomy, science, law or philosophy. It might name a revered classical historical figure directly or refer indirectly to their branch of knowledge and discovery.

Structure

The dramatic structure of your play might adopt a classical model; for example, the five-act structure. The drama genres of tragedy and comedy often drew upon traditional classical models; for example, the tragedy of the individual or revenge tragedy. The use of classical genres provides literary contexts for some of the character types in your play; for example, the tragic hero or the revenge hero.

Dramatic conventions

Ancient Greek drama uses the convention of a Chorus who come onto the stage at the start of the play and before or after key scenes. Their role is to inform, summarise, guide and warn the audience of the fate and fortunes of the main characters and the outcomes in the plot. They highlight moral issues and dilemmas but do not judge the characters directly. You can see an example of this in the *Doctor Faustus* extract on page 29.

Settings

Setting the play in ancient Greece or the distant Mediterranean past shows us a world in which classical ideals operated. Presentations of the behaviour and values of classical characters can be compared and contrasted with characters in English or non-classical settings.

To uncover the significance of classical ideals in your play, the important thing is to start with the text and then move to the context. Find out what is there, how it works and why it matters in your play. The references in your play will lead you to the ways in which the classical ideals were embraced by Elizabethan and Jacobean dramatists.

Activity 2

Making sense of classical references

You do not need to overemphasise the significance of classical references.

One way to embed their relevance to the study of your plays is to keep a log.

1. As you go through the play and this book, note the significant classical references in your play.

2. Consider when and why they appear in that episode of the drama.

3. Explore how they each offer contexts on the dramatic use of symbol, language, structure, dramatic conventions and setting.

4. Consider the ways in which the classical references reveal any Elizabethan or Jacobean political, social, cultural and literary contexts in your play.

5. After you complete your log at the end of the play, see if any overall patterns emerge in the use of the references. What are your overall conclusions about the use of classical references and the Elizabethan and Jacobean cultural context of classical ideals in your play?

Ideas of humanism

You know that tension arose between the old religious certainties of medieval Catholicism and the Renaissance spirit of enquiry. Combined with Elizabethan reverence and enthusiasm for a pre-Christian world of gods and myths, the desire to find a new way of thinking or ideology led to a belief in humanism: our human ability to reason. The idea that you could understand things through a thorough and rounded education, an increased knowledge of the world and a rational thought process was compelling for many sections of Renaissance society.

This view especially appealed to scholars and intellectuals, increasingly interested in the ancient – especially Greek – philosophers. The Renaissance belief in human reason linked with ideas of controlling your own destiny.

However, England was a Christian country that believed in the power and the existence of God, the Devil, Heaven and Hell – hence the tension. So Life and the meaning of Life was a puzzle, if an interesting and exciting one, for Renaissance Man – as it had been for the Greek and Roman philosophers, and still is for us today.

Links

For more information, see Chapter 5, 'Aristotle and the Greeks' (page 34); 'Greek contexts in Elizabethan and Jacobean tragedy' (page 36); 'What the Romans did for us' (page 37).

The notion of 'Renaissance Man'

The contexts of classical ideals and humanism are evident in the notion of a Renaissance Man: one who is educated and capable of turning his mind or talent to whatever he chooses or needs. An artist can be a scientist. A musician can be a mathematician. An inventor can be a poet. A poet can be a playwright. A dramatist can write tragedy and comedy. In turn, drama can explore all the possibilities that existed for Renaissance Man. A character presented as a Renaissance Man can be in conflict with himself, torn as he is between the two worlds: the medieval one that his society is leaving behind and the modern one he has not yet fully discovered but seeks, assisted by both his classical scholarship and his humanist ideas. Conflicts within Renaissance Man is a key context in many of the plays you will study from this period.

Renaissance drama

Consider these extracts from two Elizabethan plays. The first is from Shakespeare's *Hamlet* and contemplates the meaning of life. It was first printed in 1603 but was probably being performed by 1600, on the cusp between the Elizabethan and Jacobean eras. The second is earlier, from Marlowe's *Doctor Faustus*, not published until 1604 but performed from about 1588, at the height of the Elizabethan Renaissance. In the Prologue, the introduction to his title character's achievements, limitations and ambitions, Marlowe also contemplates what makes man.

Text extract 1

Hamlet

Hamlet is speaking to Rosencrantz and Guildenstern

What a piece of work is a man, how noble in reason, how infinite in faculties, in form and moving how express and admirable, in action how like an angel, in apprehension how like a god: the beauty of the world, the paragon of animals! And yet, to me, what is this quintessence of dust?

Hamlet by William Shakespeare (1603). Act 2, Scene 2, lines 304–308

Text extract 2
Doctor Faustus
The Chorus is speaking to the audience
Enter Chorus

CHORUS
Not marching now in fields of Trasimene
Where Mars did mate the Carthaginians,
Nor sporting in the dalliance of love
In courts of kings where state is overturned,
Nor in the pomp of proud audacious deeds,
Intends our muse to daunt his heavenly verse.
Only this, gentlemen: we must perform
The form of Faustus' fortunes, good or bad.
To patient judgements we appeal our plaud,
And speak for Faustus in his infancy.
Now he is born, his parents base of stock,
In Germany, within a town called Rhode.
Of riper years to Wittenberg he went,
Whereas his kinsmen chiefly brought him up.
So soon he profits in divinity,
The fruitful plot of scholarism graced,
That shortly he was graced with doctor's name,
Excelling all whose sweet delight disputes
In heavenly matters of theology;
Till, swoll'n with cunning of a self-conceit,
His waxen wings did mount above his reach,
And melting heavens conspired his overthrow.
For, falling to a devilish exercise,
And glutted more with learning's golden gifts,
He surfeits upon cursed necromancy;
Nothing so sweet as magic is to him,
Which he prefers before his chiefest bliss.
And this the man that in his study sits.

Exit

Doctor Faustus by Christopher Marlowe.
Prologue, lines 1–28 of the 'A text' (lines 1–27 of the 'B text')

Applying context questions 1

Linking Renaissance texts and contexts
Answer the following questions:

1. How do Shakespeare and Marlowe explore ideas about the concept of Renaissance Man?

2. How do these two extracts demonstrate to you the significance of the Renaissance contexts in Elizabethan and Jacobean drama?

3. Identify examples of extracts from your own plays that demonstrate the importance of Renaissance contexts.

Links

For more information, see Chapter 10, 'The dramatic significance of Italy': 'The role of Italy' (page 90); 'The dramatic use of travel and exotica': 'The Renaissance and the unknown' (page 91); 'How to contextualise the setting's in your play': 'William Shakespeare, *The Tempest*' (page 95).

Link

For more information, see Chapter 11, 'The significance of indoor and outdoor spaces' (page 100).

The interest in foreign travel

You know that the Renaissance was a time of foreign expansionism. The establishment of colonies across the globe, especially in the Americas, and the trade routes being opened beyond Europe into Africa and Asia reveal a thirst for an even bigger world than the one previously available to a pre-Renaissance society.

The idea of a bigger world and its accompanying navigational knowledge provided an expansion of horizons in two senses. Firstly, the people of the Renaissance had discovered that there was more to know and find out if they went beyond their own home and country. Secondly, sections of Renaissance society brought into their own homes and circles some of the ideas, beliefs and domestic produce of the places they had been – bringing the expanded horizon to the people who could not visit the distant lands.

England developed a concept of the exotic. Those who could travel did. Renaissance travellers were most likely soldiers, seamen, merchants, scholars and the rich.

There were pitfalls. England exported the attitudes of an English supremacy which believed that, because we built a ship and pursued a colonial ambition, we were superior to societies which did not. This export created a set of problems that the world has paid for ever since. The idea of problematic attitudes towards non-English peoples and places has been presented, consciously or otherwise, in many of the plays you study, as an ambivalent attraction and suspicion towards foreign exotica.

The widespread English theatre scene

Whilst travel was restricted to those with wealth, opportunity or a travelling occupation, the English Renaissance saw an unprecedented interest in going to the theatre. It was special because it crossed social class, occupation, education and personal wealth. Plays were not only attended by the aristocracy and landed gentry but also entertained (and instructed) the English peasants and artisans. Plays were enthusiastically received by monarchy at Court and funded by both Elizabeth I and James I. Drama was performed indoors and outdoors. It was the entertainment of choice in specially built theatre-houses. There were travelling shows in villages and market squares across the country.

The theatre was the place to be, the social activity of the day. The playwrights were fully aware of the broad appeal of the theatre and the all-encompassing nature of the audiences for whom they wrote. Accordingly, they crafted dramatic action, plots and language which worked both at a sophisticated and scholarly level and also at a cruder slapstick or violent level. As a result, no one from the Elizabethan and Jacobean audience was left unmoved by the fortunes of the characters. How do you think the broad social appeal of the theatre during this period compares with its popularity in your own society?

A PLAY IN A LONDON INN YARD, IN THE TIME OF QUEEN ELIZABETH.

Outdoor performance of a play in an Elizabethan inn-yard

English playwrights and their plays

What have you learned about your plays so far? Are they Elizabethan or Jacobean? How do they:

- reflect the historical and political conflicts and rebellions of the time? Is this revealed in the text directly or indirectly?

- explore contemporary attitudes towards revenge and punishment?

- demonstrate the contexts of the Renaissance?

- explore ideas about the Renaissance Man?

- reveal contemporary religious ideas?

- embody classical ideals?

Now consider another play: *The Spanish Tragedy* by Thomas Kyd.

Applying contexts to text

The Spanish Tragedy was first printed in 1592 but was performed several years earlier. It was so famous it was known as 'Hieronimo's play' (the tragic hero of the drama, a Spanish nobleman). It was even quoted in other plays as one that everyone knew.

The plot is intricate. Chapter 12 gives you a basic outline. The following extract begins just as Hieronimo finishes recounting the terrible events to the King of Spain, in a 79-line speech. It is from the penultimate scene of the play.

> ### Links
>
> For more information, see Chapter 3, 'Biographical contexts' (pages 18–19), Chapter 6, 'The use of sources' (page 45) and Chapter 13, 'Chronology of events' (pages 107–108).

Text extract 3

The Spanish Tragedy

HIERONIMO

And gentles, thus I end my play:
Urge no more words: I have no more to say.
He runs to hang himself

KING

O hearken, Viceroy! Hold, Hieronimo!
Brother, my nephew and thy son are slain!

VICEROY

We are betrayed! My Balthazar is slain!
Break ope the doors, run, save Hieronimo.
[*They break in, and hold Hieronimo*]
Hieronimo, do but inform the king of these events;
Upon mine honour thou shalt have no harm.

HIERONIMO

Viceroy, I will not trust thee with my life,
Which I this day have offered to my son.
Accursed wretch,
Why stayest thou him that was resolved to die?

KING

Speak, traitor; damned, bloody murderer, speak!
For now I have thee I will make thee speak –
Why hast thou done this undeserving deed?

VICEROY

Why hast thou murdered my Balthazar?

CASTILE

Why hast thou butchered both my children thus?

HIERONIMO

O, good words!
As dear to me was my Horatio
As yours, or yours, my lord, to you.

My guiltless son was by Lorenzo slain,
And by Lorenzo and that Balthazar
Am I at last revenged thoroughly,
Upon whose souls may heavens be yet avenged
With greater far than these afflictions.

CASTILE

But who were thy confederates in this?

VICEROY

That was thy daughter Bel-Imperia;
For by her hand my Balthazar was slain:
I saw her stab him.

KING   Why speak'st thou not?

HIERONIMO

What lesser liberty can kings afford
Than harmless silence? Then afford it me:
Sufficeth I may not, nor I will not tell thee.

KING

Fetch forth the tortures.
Traitor as thou art, I'll make thee tell.

HIERONIMO   Indeed,
Thou may'st torment me, as his wretched son
Hath done in murdering my Horatio,
But never shalt thou force me to reveal
The thing which I have vowed inviolate.
And therefore in despite of all thy threats,
Pleased with their deaths, and eased with revenge,
First take my tongue, and afterwards my heart.
[*He bites out his tongue*]

The Spanish Tragedy by Thomas Kyd (1592).
Act 4, Scene 4, lines 151–191

Summary

This chapter has introduced you to the world outside of the plays and the significance of historical and political, social and cultural contexts in your study of Elizabethan and Jacobean drama. You should now have more knowledge of:

- ruling English monarchs 1590–1640
- Renaissance beliefs and ideas
- English playwrights and their plays
- applying contexts to text, including your own plays.

Applying context questions 2

Exploring text for contexts

1. Identify the ways in which Kyd dramatises his contemporary historical and political, social and cultural contexts of revenge, punishment, conflicts and rebellions. Consider Kyd's use of language and dramatic techniques.

2. Identify how your play(s) dramatise the contexts above.

3. Link Kyd's use of a) contexts and b) language/dramatic techniques to the ending or closing scenes of your own play(s). Identify the features that appear in both your play and Kyd's. Compare and contrast their purpose in the texts and effects on the audience.

5 Literary contexts

The dramatic genres of tragedy, history and comedy

These genres do not begin or end with the Elizabethan and Jacobean period – as you will see, their history is long – nor are these only English genres. The popularity of tragedy is particularly significant in this period and will receive the most detailed treatment of the three in this chapter.

Comedy within tragedy
Comic relief

One genre can use the dramatic conventions of another genre. The use of comic features within a tragedy is part of its dramatic structure. The comic scenes provide comic relief for the audience from the main tragic plot, to interrupt the tense or sombre mood of the play by lightening the tone. The mood change of comedy within tragedy contributes to the structure of the play by altering the pace of the action.

The structural and tone shifts created from comic relief scenes can have two effects on you, the audience. One is to provide a **distraction** from the main themes and ideas in the play to take your mind off the tragedy momentarily so that the sorrow, horror or catastrophe does not feel unrelenting. The other is to reflect on the main plot, themes and ideas to **amplify** their dramatic significance as you pause for thought, either through laughter or comparison with the serious events.

For example, in *Doctor Faustus*, when Marlowe presents Robin the clown conjuring up Mephistopheles, the scene echoes an earlier one where Faustus has done the same, signing his soul away to the Devil as part of his over-reaching and fatal ambition. In *Hamlet*, the grave-diggers' conversation about Ophelia's burial and suicide is a comment on the Christian views of suicide at the time. In both of these cases, the dramatist gives the comic episode a moral significance. The audience is encouraged to consider the rights and wrongs of the event, ideas or behaviour that the comedy is underlining in the tragic main plot.

Horrid laughter

Jacobean tragedies often use comedy in a grim and macabre way, embedded within the dramatic mood and the tragic events in the plot rather than in separate comic scenes. Sometimes referred to as 'horrid laughter', the hero (or main characters) mocks or parodies the brutal acts in the play, even as he commits them himself, as part of a grimacing, cackling humour.

For example: in Middleton's *The Revenger's Tragedy* with Vindice and his duplicitous murder of the Duke, and in Webster's *The White Devil*, as Francisco plots his revenge he tells the audience that 'My tragedy must have some idle mirth in 't' (Act 4, Scene 1, line 118). An indifference to violence is conveyed to the audience and the casual or frenzied tone of murder and cruelty appears more shocking for appearing so trivialised.

Chapter aims

In this chapter we will examine a specific aspect of literary contexts: genre. The dramatic genre is divided into three further main genres:

- tragedy
- history
- comedy.

Think about it

Comedy within tragedy
How does your tragedy use comic relief or/and 'horrid laughter' in the structure and mood of the play? What is the dramatic significance of its use in your play?

Your dramatist and genre

These dramatists each wrote in more than one genre. Some have a preference and are remembered and studied for one particular genre. Marlowe is famous for his tragedies and some histories. Jonson's comedies are widely studied but he also wrote tragedy. Shakespeare prolifically wrote equally in all three. The Jacobean drama by Middleton, Webster or Ford is tragedy, although each of them wrote comedies. We consider only a fraction of each one's output.

Analysing genre as context

As we consider each genre, we will look at:

- useful definitions and their origins

- Elizabethan and Jacobean subgenres

- contextual applications to your drama texts.

Tragedy
Defining tragedy

Tragedy can generally be defined as a form of drama concerned with human suffering. This definition was refined by the Ancient Greeks. In terms of influence on this period, tragedy began with the Ancient Greeks.

Aristotle and the Greeks

Aristotle, an Ancient Greek philosopher from the 4th century BC, developed definitions and theories on many philosophical questions that we still ask today. Among these questions was: 'What is tragedy?' Here is a summary of Aristotle's definition of tragedy:

Tragedy is the **acting out** of a deed of great importance which has serious consequences. The deed, or action, is expressed and enriched through the language but the key is to enact the tragedy and not simply recite it as poetry. The audience experiences strong emotions which move through pity and fear to a kind of relief at the end, when it is over – a purging and then healing of the emotions felt throughout the enactment of the tragedy.

Catharsis is dependent not only upon the actors, the **enactment** of the tragedy, but also on the **reception** of the tragedy: you, and your emotional response to what you witness and experience. Aristotle understood that the audience is a vital component of the tragedy. Ask yourself: would I feel the same way as the characters if I was in their shoes? If the answer to this question is 'yes', then you feel sympathy with the characters, their tale and the outcome. Sympathising with the person whose deed is central to the tragedy is vital to the fulfilment of the tragedy genre.

The tragic hero

Aristotle theorised upon the presentation of the central character – the hero – and the main deed – the plot. He said that tragedy is defined by a serious and dignified tone through the hero and the plot. The hero should be a great and important person, usually a king or aristocrat, whose fortunes go from good to bad during the play. We call this the **reversal of fortune**. This reversal must also be caused by the hero himself, through a mistake he makes that cannot be undone. He commits an action, or actions, that cause his reversal, or downfall. The Greeks called this mistake hamartia.

Remember

Catharsis

Catharsis is the Greek name for purging and healing of the emotions as the drama ends. For the Greeks, achieving catharsis was vital for the definition and enactment of tragedy.

Link

For more information, see Chapter 3, 'The genre': The "realisable" text' (page 14) and 'Open to reception and interpretation' (page 17).

Key term

Hamartia the fatal flaw (or mistake) of a tragic hero.

The English translation of hamartia is 'flaw', something in the hero's character that causes his behaviour and is responsible for his mistakes. The English definition implies a moral weakness, as if the mistake would always be made, given his character. The Greek definition – of a mistake – implies an element of misjudgement which is then paid for eternally in the world of the play and its characters. The difference is subtle, but interesting. The Greek meaning suggests that the mistake issues a disproportionate consequence – this might affect the Greek approach to 'sympathy'. The English version, adapted into Elizabethan tragedy, appears harsher. It suggests that there was no chance of any other outcome: it is down to the individual and their personal flaws.

Ultimately, the outcome is the same: the downfall of the hero is inevitable and caused, in part, by his own doing. The element of inevitability is what makes the tragedy and is a key component of the **tragic hero**.

Responding to the tragic hero
It is essential that we are not left feeling that the tragic hero is merely a blundering fool or catharsis will not occur. It is usual for the tragic hero to achieve some self-awareness by the end of the play. He must take responsibility for his own part in the tragedy and how that led to the tragic outcome. Whether he comes to grasp the will of the gods or some truth about human limitation and destiny, he must experience some revelation which changes him and restores dignity to his character. This occurs just before he dies – which he must, as an inevitable consequence of his hamartia. This revelation is his 'light-bulb' moment. The Greeks called this anagnorisis.

Responding to the tragic outcome
The anagnorisis of the tragic hero ensures that the audience is not left feeling that the suffering was in vain or that the revelation came too late to be of use. It is not about regret – that if only the hero had realised earlier the potential outcome of his actions, there would be no tragedy. There is no 'happy ever after' for the characters of a Greek tragedy. They all suffer from the hero's hamartia, owing to his status and influence on the world in which he operates. The point of the tragedy is for the audience to learn something about human behaviour and the human condition.

The importance of tragic inevitability
This definition means that accidents, unfortunate events or events caused by others and external forces do not make a tragedy in the Greek mode. They may be sad but they are misadventures, not tragedies, as there is no tragic inevitability to the story. Similarly, social drama which depicts a character as a victim of circumstances is not a tragedy in this Greek mould as it depends entirely on the world in which the character finds him or herself. If he or she was put somewhere else, given a fresh start, his or her predicament might become irrelevant and no tragedy would ensue. This approach recalls the phrase 'there but for fortune go I' rather than the inevitability caused by the deeper motivations of human behaviour, be they psychological or religious. Your grasp of the Aristotelian theory of tragedy cannot be underestimated in your study of an Elizabethan or Renaissance tragedy.

Heroes in modern tragedy
If you have some knowledge of how the hero (or heroine) is constructed or perceived in social drama – such as the tragedies of Henrik Ibsen, Arthur

Did you know?

Greek etymology of 'hamartia'
The word traces from 'hamartanein', a sporting term for when an archer or spear-thrower misses his target.

The status of the tragic hero
Sophocles and Aeschylus wrote about kings in *Oedipus Rex* and *Agamemnon* respectively. Euripides wrote about the tragedy of women, the old and slaves in *Medea*, and criticised the Greek glorification of war in *The Trojan Women*. Euripides was mocked for his social attitudes, in Greek comedies by Aristophanes such as *The Frogs*.

Think about it

Hamartia: 'flaw' or 'mistake'?
How does the English translation fit with the 'Renaissance world' views, of shifting religious beliefs and the ideas of humanism, explored in Chapter 4?

Key term

Anagnorisis the moment the tragic hero realises that his flaw has partly caused the tragedy.

Examiner's tip

Contextualising tragedy
Ensure that you understand the conventions and terms of tragedy before you write about it.

Do not confuse the terms 'tragedy', 'tragic' and 'hero' with other popular, non-literary, meanings.

Further reading

The importance of the Greeks

- http://anarchon.tripod.com/indexGREEKTH.html: This accessible webpage is written by a teacher. It provides an excellent introduction for students who want a more detailed guide to the history of Greek theatre.

- Aristotle, *Poetics*, for his theories of tragedy.

- The tragedies of Aeschylus, Sophocles and Euripides.

Link

For more information, see Chapter 4, 'The Renaissance context': 'The influence of classical ideals' (page 26) and 'Ideas of humanism' (page 27).

Remember

Subgenres in a tragedy

Just as a tragedy can have comic elements, it can have elements of more than one subgenre. For example, it might draw on ideas about domestic tragedy and features of revenge tragedy.

Miller or J.B. Priestley – you might wonder how Aristotle's theory fits these plays. You might notice how different they are from the Elizabethan and Jacobean plays in their presentations of a tragic hero and would be right to suggest that they do not fit very well into the Greek model. The reason is that they have different historical, social, cultural and literary contexts because they were conceived in an entirely different world, that of the 20th century. The changing interpretations over time, of ideas about the tragic hero, demonstrate how 20th- and 21st-century receptions of tragedy can evolve or depart from earlier models in response to our own contexts.

Greek contexts in Elizabethan and Jacobean tragedy

The Greek definition has significance for all Elizabethan and some Jacobean tragedy. Aristotle's philosophical enquiry into tragedy struck a chord with Renaissance development and definitions of Western civilisation. Despite the time difference, there is a clear link between how Aristotle and the Ancient Greeks viewed tragedy and how the Elizabethans and some Jacobeans viewed tragedy. We get an artistic and historical continuity between two very different worlds: the pagan Hellenes and the Christian English. The English Renaissance embodies this continuity and the classical dramatic tradition is part of what was being celebrated at that time. We still make these links today. For example, some of you will be studying paired texts – of Greek drama, such as Sophocles' *Oedipus Rex*, and Shakespeare, such as *King Lear*.

The tragedy of the individual

The main tragedians from the period who use the Greek definition and model are Marlowe (Elizabethan) and Shakespeare (Elizabethan and Jacobean). Adapting this model to their own Renaissance world and beliefs, they wrote what we now call the **tragedy of the individual**. These tragedies depict the reversal of fortune of a tragic hero: an individual man of importance whose hamartia leads to his inevitable downfall. In each case, at the end, the hero demonstrates anagnorisis and the audience experiences catharsis.

Domestic tragedy

The Jacobean playwrights (Middleton, Webster and Ford) wrote what we might now classify as **domestic tragedy**. These differ from the tragedy of the individual in that the tragic hero is not a king, aristocrat or singularly important person such as a prestigious scholar or a military general. Usually, the tragic hero is a middle-class person or an outsider within their own society (rather than a very powerful man or ruler) who has somehow distinguished him or herself from the ordinary populace. Sometimes the hero is a woman and possibly still an aristocrat.

Activity 1

Classifying your tragedies

1. Which do you think can be contextualised as a) a tragedy of the individual and b) a domestic tragedy? In each case, explain how.

2. Which ones do you think are hard to classify? Why?

Performing Greek tragedy

The Athenians, in their Golden Age of the 5th century BC, performed to huge audiences.

The amphitheatre at Athens was built outdoors on a hillside. Performances lasted all day and were usually structured as a trilogy of tragedies, finishing with a comic piece (a 'satyr'). The event was often a competition in which three playwrights each had the stage for a whole day. The goal was dramatic glory. The setting was an annual festival in honour of the god of fertility, Dionysus. A Greek chorus not only sang its commentary but also danced. All actors were men and each wore a mask to depict the emotions of their individual character. The event was a visual spectacle. The performance was open to all – even women!

Did you know?

The amphitheatre of Dionysus
The amphitheatre at Athens seated audiences of 15,000. Our modern equivalents are football and rugby stadiums – or as the Greeks would say, stadia – designed for huge, communal outdoor events and big emotions.

The remains of the ancient theatre of Dionysus in Athens on the slope of the Acropolis

Activity 2

Comparing performance styles

1. Can you make any links between the performance of tragedy in Ancient Greece and the ways in which your plays might have been performed in the Elizabethan and Jacobean period?

2. How important is the contemporary setting or design in the performance of your plays, then and now?

Links

For more information, see Chapter 9, 'Boy players' and 'Acting styles' (page 79) and Chapter 11, 'The significance of indoor and outdoor spaces' (page 100).

We have focused on how Greek tragedy influenced Elizabethan and Jacobean tragedy, especially the tragedies of Shakespeare and Marlowe. Let us explore some other influences.

What the Romans did for us
Seneca and Greek tragedy

As the Roman Empire expanded into Greece in the 3rd century BC, the Romans were exposed to Greek tragedy. They performed Greek tragedy

Seneca, Roman tragedian and Stoic

but began writing their own Roman tragedies. The most famous Roman tragedian is **Seneca**, a philosopher, who lived in the 1st century BC. Seneca was clearly influenced by the Greeks but he offered new ways to write a tragedy. For example, Senecan plays follow a five-act structure – can you compare this with any of your plays?

There are some other differences between the tragedies of Seneca and the Greeks. Seneca's style is thought now to be rather ponderous with long speeches, narrative accounts of action, general moralising on human behaviour and a rather self-conscious and formal style. Some critics and historians suggest that this is because they were intended for private recitals and not public enactments.

Whilst the gods are not a significant feature (unlike in Greek tragedy), Senecan tragedy is populated by ghosts and witches. A key feature of the Senecan plot and character motivation is revenge. These revenge tales are told through a swirl of multiple deaths by murder and suicide. Violence – although off-stage – is presented as bloody and gory, and the supernatural is ever-present. Does this sound similar to Jacobean tragedies?

Seneca and Stoicism
Seneca was a Stoic. His plays often present characters as achieving the calm for which Stoics are known, at the end of a violent and terrifying set of tragic events. The tragic hero and other characters are seen to accept pain and suffering as the just and right outcome for the events that unfold and which they cause. This relates to the anagnorisis of the Greeks but with a Roman emphasis on 'taking it on the chin'. The degree of pain that the hero suffers in punishment is a measure of the dignity that he ultimately earns.

As with the Greeks, no one escapes justice. An element of Stoic acceptance, if not exactly calm, can be seen in Shakespeare's *Macbeth*. Macbeth, the tragic hero, says to Macduff, towards the end of the play as they fight to the death, 'Lay on, Macduff'. Macbeth knows that he might die and that Macduff has been prophesied to deliver this end – which Macbeth feels, and the audience might agree, that he has made inevitable. When Macbeth says 'And damned be him that first cries, "Hold, enough!"' (meaning 'Do not dare to say, "Stop! I surrender"'), he shows that the only way out of this conflict is death, which he accepts as he is ready to endure the suffering of that end with dignity and honour.

Revenge tragedy
Senecan tragedy is a key literary context for Elizabethan and Jacobean revenge tragedy. The features that we cannot see in the Greek model often come from this Roman model. Shakespeare, Middleton, Webster and Ford all wrote revenge tragedies. The revenge subgenre has become a by-word for the period, particularly the Jacobean era, hence the phrase 'Jacobean revenge tragedy'. The defining features of a revenge tragedy are:

- a ghost appearing before a kinsman, often a son
- a secret murder, often of a fading or unpopular ruler by a person of questionable morality
- a period of disguise, intrigue or plotting – often the murderer and the avenger plot against each other

- a descent into either real or feigned madness by the avenger or one of the minor characters
- characters are killed and grisly deaths – vengeful or accidental – come to dominate the plot
- a frenzied outcome of all-encompassing violence – often this occurs during a party or celebration, controlled in part by the hopeful avenger
- the final outcome wipes out many of the cast, including – significantly – the avenger.

Activity 3

Revenge tragedy

1. Which of your plays can be contextualised as a revenge tragedy or one that draws on some significant elements of the subgenre?

2. What – possibly moral – questions are being explored through the use of this subgenre?

3. What are the plays telling us about the society in which they were written and performed?

4. How do your plays change features of the subgenre to ask questions about human behaviour and morality? Why?

Exploring revenge tragedy

Hamlet subverts the subgenre of revenge tragedy to probe the psychological motivations of a man, Prince Hamlet, torn between his duties to revenge his father's unjust death and his belief in Renaissance Christian morality. Shakespeare weaves together the Greek and Roman literary contexts to question our morality and human behaviour.

An example of a Jacobean revenge tragedy which begins to deviate from the strict conventions is Middleton's *The Revenger's Tragedy*. The play seems to mock not only the genre of revenge – with its skull used as a 'talking head' and the skeleton dressed as a bride – but also Shakespeare's *Hamlet* and Prince Hamlet himself. Middleton's avenger, Vindice (which even means 'avenger') seems to laugh at Hamlet's delay. We see a contrast with Hamlet's procrastination when Vindice cries 'hurry, hurry, hurry!' (Act 2, Scene 1, line 200), as if Hamlet is simply wasting time by not rushing to his revenge. *The Revenger's Tragedy* is a gutsy, pacey, rude, comic, even funny exploration of revenge and its consequences.

Webster uses revenge tragedy in further radical ways. He (almost like Euripides the Greek) challenges the patriarchal traditions to probe some class, race and gender issues through his plots and characterisations. He does not give us high-status, male, tragic heroes. *The White Devil* and *The Duchess of Malfi* demonstrate how Webster uses strong female characters as his **protagonists**. Our latest example of the period is Ford. Like Middleton and Webster, he emphasised the frenzy of revenge. In his play *'Tis Pity She's a Whore*, Ford ratchets-up the shock factor through revenge plots that revolve around incest, between the crazed Giovanni and his doomed sister Annabella.

> **Key term**
>
> **Protagonist** the principal character in the play.

Some questions about the tragedy genre

- How might you better understand the contexts of a Jacobean tragedy now that you have grasped some principles of Greek and Roman tragedy? (A good example might be Webster's tragedies.)

- How could you use Activities 1 and 2 to contextualise *The Duchess of Malfi*? (If you don't know the play, the title will give you some information.) How might those classifications and performance styles have limited use as you contextualise this play?

- What does this tell you about some of the differences between Shakespeare and Webster? They both write in the same genre, tragedy. Explore how Webster adapts little of the Greek model and relies more on other types of tragedy within his work.

- Middleton and Ford barely use the Greek model. What do these Jacobeans do instead? Where do their genre influences – their literary contexts – come from?

- Is Shakespeare only interested in the Greek model? Does he use features of other types of tragedy, shared with Jacobean dramatists? Does he use these shared features only in his later, Jacobean, tragedies or also in his earlier, Elizabethan, ones?

It might appear that the Jacobean revenge tragedies are more risky and socially challenging than the Elizabethan Renaissance tragedies. In other ways, the Jacobeans might seem less challenging than the Elizabethans in their dramatic craft and technical innovations. However, you can see that tragedy is at the heart of Elizabethan and Jacobean drama. In some ways, it is the dominant genre of its period – often breast-beating and blood-thirsty.

History

The Jacobean dramatists did write history plays but you are far more likely to study their tragedies. The history plays you study are likely to be written by Shakespeare and Marlowe. There are three history play subgenres to consider:

- English histories
- ancient histories
- tragic histories.

Definitions and subgenres

English histories

Elizabethan and Jacobean English history plays often acted as military or royal propaganda as well as a dramatic representation of historical events. They are concerned with the machinations of state and the world of kings and the court, usually during wartime or political rebellion. Deeds are fictionalised or embellished and edited to present a patriotic or critical view of kingship and rule. Examples include Shakespeare's *Henry V*.

Ancient histories

Examples of these include Shakespeare's *Antony and Cleopatra* and Marlowe's *Tamburlaine the Great*. Each is concerned with the significant history of a ruler from the classical or European/Asian past. The first is

---

Think about it

Tragedy: individual or revenge?

Consider what you know about the differences between Elizabethan and Jacobean society: the contrasting political, social and cultural contexts operating in their worlds. Why might one society produce more **tragedies of the individual**, based on a Greek model, and the other produce more **revenge tragedies**, based on a Roman model?

Think about it

English history plays

Why do you think Shakespeare and Marlowe set their English history plays in the past? Why did they not write one called 'Elizabeth I' or 'James I'?

famous as a tragic love story. The second is an example of an epic and is also a tragedy. Other ancient history plays, for example *Titus Andronicus*, are examples of revenge tragedy. What unites these histories as a subgenre is that they are set in the distant past with characters from history.

Tragic histories
The tragic history subgenre should be studied and analysed as tragedy. You can use the earlier section on tragedy to contextualise this subgenre. Tragic histories might focus on the rule of a real king or aristocrat from English or Scottish history, but it is the tragedy, the fortunes and hamartia of the tragic hero that drives the play and its outcome to the same audience catharsis as the other tragedies. Examples are Shakespeare's *Macbeth* and *Richard II* and Marlowe's *Edward II*. Like the individual tragedies they centre on the reversal of fortune of an important figure, which ends not only in their untimely death but in the murder of those who surround them. The murders are often gruesome and share features of revenge tragedy.

Comedy
Defining comedy
Comedy can generally be defined as a form of drama with a happy or satisfying outcome for the plot and its main characters. The audience might laugh at the end of, and during, the drama but the main aim is for the characters and the plot to be happily resolved in their narratives and relationships. We call the happy ending a **comic resolution**. You might not laugh but you might smile or feel content that the characters survive mostly unharmed. Serious moral issues can be aired and taught to the audience through comedy in either a light-hearted or tense way.

Elizabethan and Jacobean comedy
Instead of dying, romance blooms, festivities abound and characters usually get married after a period of difficulty or separation, often caused by mistaken identity or a misunderstanding. They are often assisted by a clever servant, sometimes known as the fool – which he never is – or a mischief-maker, the clown. In other cases, it is a matter of comic justice, in which characters get what they are seen to deserve and conventional society is protected from their attempted villainy, mischief or buffoonery. Such characters will be made a 'laughing stock' or chastised.

Restoring order
By the end of the comedy, the audience is presented with a fair and just world where the 'good' or innocent characters are rewarded and the 'bad' or guilty characters, sometimes the deceitful ones, are humiliated and punished. They are not killed, as their crimes or misdeeds are usually misdemeanours that can be overcome, not irreversible mistakes doomed to stain humanity eternally. Order, hierarchy and old certainties are restored after a rocky patch of disturbance and uncertainty. Any perceived imbalance in the accepted social order, or attempt to rock the boat, in the eyes of Elizabethan or Jacobean audiences will rarely triumph at the outcome.

Subversive elements of comedy
Comedy in this period might introduce subversive themes and characterisations – often delivered through rude and bawdy language or

Key term

Epic celebrates the feats of a hero, often legendary, in a similar style and structure to a long narrative poem.

Think about it

Issues of succession in the histories
Why do you think so many Elizabethan plays are about kings and kingship, rulers and ruling and challenges to the royal dynasty?

Did you know?

Sources of the plays
Dramatists of the Elizabethan and Jacobean period rarely invented a plot from scratch. As well as tales from history, they used existing chronicles – for example, Holinshed's – and also fictional stories. They adapted poetry or myth and even rewrote earlier dramas. They showed that the power of a tale is in its telling and use of genre. They re-worked the source into something of contemporary relevance in the play.

Link

For more information, see Chapter 8, 'Significant character types in context' (page 66).

Remember

Comedy from this period
The only character who pays for his or her wrong-doings is the one who committed them, punished by the trusted guardians in authority – a far cry from the consequences of the wrong-doings in a tragedy.

cross-dressing escapades and naughty fairies – but the genre produces outcomes that ultimately toe the social line. The main characters live happily ever after, or at least are conventionally settled, in state-approved institutions (like marriage) accepting the state-approved structures of religion, family, law and governance. By the end, smart women, ambitious servants, disruptive creatures from the supernatural and fantasy worlds do not control the social status quo. If this all sounds a bit too serious, consider your own comedies. The entertainment is designed to bring you fun and pleasure rather than the pain and suffering of the tragedy. Matters of great importance are rarely risked, foiled or achieved, even when serious moral issues are under consideration.

Activity 4

What's in your comedy?
How far do these statements and ideas about comedy and this summary of comic conventions apply to your plays?

'Sympathy' in comedy

Sympathy for characters is limited in comedy. Because the events can never become too unpredictable, the audience must not get attached to the motivations and presentation of any particular character. You can be encouraged to root for or against them but the nature of a comic plot determines that you cannot care too much for their fortunes, or it will be hard for you to let go and laugh at their misfortunes if they fall.

Stock characters

Comedy relies on stock characters, a set of stereotypes who the audience can respond to superficially as ones that we know will behave in a certain way. Despite the inevitability that we find in tragedy, because the characters are often presented as complex compared with the simplicity of comic characters, the characters of a comedy are usually far more predictable in their actions. For example, the lovers are usually young and beautiful in a comedy. They can be cheeky, saucy or graceful depending on the nature of the lovers' relationship and the execution of the plot to unite them in love. They may rampage around the set but at the end of the play the most radical thing they do is get married. We know this will be the outcome so never have to worry about a happy ending for them.

Comic resolution and the plot

The variety of presentations of human qualities, and the moods to which they contribute in the play, allows an intricacy to develop in the plot and often several subplots. Such intricacy makes it appear that several things could go wrong and that several outcomes are possible. However, the audience knows it is watching a comedy and not a tragedy and that only one outcome is possible: comic resolution.

Comic subgenres

You can divide the comedies that you might encounter from this period into two subgenres: pastoral and city.

Pastoral comedies

Shakespeare wrote many pastoral comedies based either in rural settings or on the shifting tensions between the natural world and the world of the court. These are more typical of the Elizabethan era.

City comedies

Jonson wrote city comedies set in the seedier worlds of London and Venice, populated by more dubious shades of characters. These are more typical of the Jacobean era. City comedies are more cynical in their approach to character, mood and plot outcome, relying more on baser human instincts and desires.

Whichever subgenre of Elizabethan or Jacobean comedy you are watching, you can enjoy all comic styles: slapstick, puns, sarcasm, sexual innuendo, wit and practical jokes.

Tragi-comedy

Several of Shakespeare's comedies, such as *Measure for Measure* and *The Tempest*, present us with an uncomfortable mix of comedy and tragedy. They begin with a problem of such gravity that we anticipate a tragic outcome even though comic elements are present from the outset. However, they have a comic resolution where order is restored happily rather than with the sorrow or calamity of the tragedy, and all the loose ends are tied. Despite this, some audience members might still leave with a nagging doubt about whether the right thing has been done. As a result, we classify them as 'problem' plays.

How to compare tragic and comic outcomes

Applying context questions 1

Comparative analysis of comic and tragic endings
Read the extracts on the following page. One is a tragedy and the other is a comedy. For each:

- Identify the genre. Identify the subgenre. How did you do this?

- Identify the tragic characters. Identify the comic characters. Identify the mood. How does their dialogue and language contribute to the tragic or comic mood?

- Comment on any contextually significant aspects or features of each plot and setting.

- Comment on the contextual significance of the language.

- Identify any macro – historical and political, social and cultural – contexts. Consider their significance in each extract.

Think about it

From the palace to the forest and back
In *As You Like It* and *A Midsummer Night's Dream*, Shakespeare shifts between two contrasting settings of the forest and the palace – why?

Remember

City comedy
The 'city' subgenre is closely linked to satire.

Key term

Satire ironic comedy used to mock and judge people, groups or organisations and their vices – for example, vulgar greed.

Think about it

Tragi-comedy
Is the 'problem' that we cannot accept the Elizabethan moral solutions to the problems in the plot? Or that Shakespeare subverts and merges the genres themselves?

The masks of Comedy and Tragedy

Extract 1
Exton delivers Richard II's corpse to Bullingbrook
Enter Exton with a coffin
EXTON
Great king, within this coffin I present
Thy buried fear. Herein all breathless lies
The mightiest of thy greatest enemies,
Richard of Bordeaux, by me hither brought.

BULLINGBROOK
Exton, I thank thee not, for thou hast wrought
A deed of slander with thy fatal hand
Upon my head and all this famous land.

EXTON
From your own mouth, my lord, did I this deed.

BULLINGBROOK
They love not poison that do poison need.
Nor do I thee. Though I did wish him dead,
I hate the murderer, love him murdered.
The guilt of conscience take thou for thy labour,
But neither my good word nor princely favour.
With Cain go wander through shades of night
And never show thy head by day or night.
Lords, I protest my soul is full of woe
That blood should sprinkle me to make me grow.
Come mourn with me for what I do lament,
And put on sullen black incontinent
I'll make a voyage to the Holy Land
To wash this blood off from my guilty hand.
March sadly after. Grace my mournings here
In weeping after this untimely bier.

Exeunt

Extract 2
Oberon, the King of Fairies, addresses his train; followed by Puck, his clown
OBERON
So shall all the couples three
Ever true in loving be,
And the blots of nature's hand
Shall not in their issue stand.
Never mole, harelip, nor scar,
Nor mark prodigious, such as are
Despised in nativity,
Shall upon their children be.
With this field-dew consecrate,
Every fairy take his gait,
And each several chamber bless
Through this palace with sweet peace;
And the owner of it blessed
Ever shall in safety rest.
Trip away, make no stay;
Meet me all by break of day.

Exeunt all but Puck

PUCK *To the audience*
If we shadows have offended,
Think but this and all is mended:
That you have all but slumbered here
Whilst these visions did appear;
And this weak and idle theme,
No more yielding but a dream,
Gentles, do not reprehend;
And, as I am an honest Puck,
If we have unearned luck
Now to 'scape the serpent's tongue
We will make amends ere long,
Else the Puck a liar call.
So, good night unto you all.
Give me your hands, if we be friends,
And Robin shall restore amends.   [*Exit*]

Summary
This chapter has introduced you to Elizabethan and Jacobean dramatic genres and subgenres. You should now have a clearer understanding of context in:
- tragedy
- history
- comedy
- tragi-comedy.

6 Plots

Defining plot

You might think that there is not much to analyse in a plot, as 'who did what when' is not the foundation for an analysis of drama in context. However, an analysis of the relationship between plot and context is important.

The plot is more than the story: plot gives the play its narrative structure. A story is descriptive and only tells you what happens and to whom. A plot is dynamic and organises the story into a structured sequence of events and actions. The execution of the plot and **how** that story is dramatised contributes to the presentation of moral, political or social messages in the play.

The use of sources

Creating a plot

The use of sources in the creation and construction of drama from this period is significant in the relationship between plot and context in your plays. The sources of a dramatic plot tell you a great deal about the influence of context on the drama and playwright at the time. This is important in the Elizabethan and the Jacobean period as it was unusual for these dramatists to invent their own stories. Our modern preoccupation with originality and imagination is a late development in the history of English literature and stems from the ideas of the Romantics at the end of the 18th century. The Elizabethans and Jacobeans did not put much of a premium on these qualities in writing.

Changing the story

The fascination of a plot does not lie in a detailed examination of centuries of documentation and their minute and complicated deviations in the storyline. It lies in exploring the **significance** of what the dramatist has omitted, added, restructured and transformed to create a new plot based on an old story.

It might also matter why a particular story is of interest to its original audiences. The shifting emphasis in the plot and the narrative structure of your plays tells you some of the thoughts and behaviour of the contemporary society in which the drama was written. It can tell you what the audience wanted, or expected, to watch on stage. You can also observe and question **how** the dramatist chose to represent those social concerns and literary fashions.

It is interesting how a tale meanders through several centuries, countries, languages, authors and genres until it arrives at your door via an Elizabethan and Jacobean dramatic version. It could have begun life as something completely different.

For example, the plot of *Hamlet* can be traced (through several sources) back to a 12th-century saga, *Amleth* (some historians believe it goes back even further to an oral tradition and a narrative that was possibly Persian or Egyptian in its origins). In the plot of 1185, Amleth survives a trip to England and his pretended madness to achieve his revenge early on in the plot. He

---

Chapter aims

In this chapter we consider the relationship between plot and context in Elizabethan and Jacobean drama. We will explore:

- a definition of plot
- the use of sources
- plot and dramatic genres
- connections between context, plot, source and genre
- the beginnings and endings of your plays.

Remember

Elizabethan and Jacobean dramatic plot sources

Fiction
- Earlier plays
- Narrative (or even lyrical) poems
- Classical stories and literature
- Myth and legend, including classical myths
- Sagas, including the Nordic sagas.

Non-fiction
- Historical chronicles, for example Holinshed's
- Documents of historical importance – for example, ship log books, records of shipwrecks
- Diaries and journals
- Essays on social matters – for example, slavery, the law, marriage.

Further reading

For plot sources of your plays

- Consult the 'Introduction' to your drama text.

  Editions listed in Chapter 14 are all highly recommended resources – scholarly, thorough and explicitly helpful on contexts and plot sources.

Classical sources

Penguin *Dictionary of Classical Mythology*

Did you know?

Elizabethan and Jacobean dramatic plots

Search online to find out how and which tales were told. Type into your web search engine: 'plot', the name of the play and the name of the dramatist. Make sure it is the dramatic plot, not the plot of a film adaptation – there may be differences in the storylines and structure of the text. (Those differences can provide further contextual information about the plots that your own society finds relevant and engaging.)

Think about it

What's in a plot?

Shakespeare's *Romeo and Juliet* and *A Midsummer Night's Dream* are basically the same story.

- What does this tell you about the relationship between plot and genre? Conversely, what are the difficulties in adapting a Jacobean revenge tragedy plot to the demands of a comedy?

- How do comic-relief scenes, or comic characters and language, contribute to tragic plots? They are always present – check your plays.

returns to rule his kingdom of Danes, reconciles with his mother and happily marries but not with Ophelia. Eventually, he dies honourably in battle – a successful, murderous warrior and king. There was originally no character of either Laertes or Fortinbras, and Polonius is unimportant in that plot.

Classical sources

Classical sources can present a hurdle as you get to grips with the language of your plays. They can be hard to avoid if they are embedded in the events of the plot. If classical sources are important to your plot, tackle a little at a time. Use the knowledge of your teachers. Read the footnotes in your play. Try to get an overall sense of how the scene or language contributes to the narrative structure. As you are not an Ancient Greek or Roman, you will not understand every reference – which does not matter.

You will extract little value from peeling away layers of literary context over thousands of years. As this book shows you, you have plenty to say about the language of your texts and the significance of context beyond what Icarus or Jove got up to. The value of understanding the use of classical sources is to help you see how a plot is constructed in a particular set of contexts.

Plot and dramatic genres
Predicting the plot

Plots can be linked to the dramatic genres of tragedy, comedy and history and their subgenres. For example, in Ford's Jacobean revenge tragedy *'Tis Pity She's a Whore*, the plot begins with a character who falls in love and has sex with his sister, whose new husband then finds out. Not surprisingly, events turn nasty and the incestuous brother descends into madness and violence as he cannot cope with the escalating outcome of his actions. You can predict that the plot is not happily resolved for the sister or anyone else caught up in their story.

Plotting the outcome

There are exceptions to this relationship between plot and genre. For example, do you know Shakespeare's tale of young, passionate lovers overcome by sexual and romantic urges to marry in secret and haste, set against a backdrop of forbidden love between feuding or incompatible families? Is that a comedy or a tragedy? It depends on how the playwright pursues the plot and orders the narrative structure. Delay the wedding, reconcile the families and reunite the lovers and you have a happy ending – a romantic, Elizabethan comedy. Marry them quickly in secret, alienate the parents and throw in revenge killings of each one's family and you have a grievous ending – a tragedy.

Plot innovation

It is interesting to look at how the playwrights develop, contradict and subvert a plot, source or subgenre to move the genre of comedy, tragedy or history into a new literary convention or era. When a dramatist transforms not only a way of creating plot but also a genre or subgenre – then he or she is not only talented and original but also an innovator. The Elizabethans – Kyd, Marlowe, Shakespeare and Jonson – are the great innovators of this period.

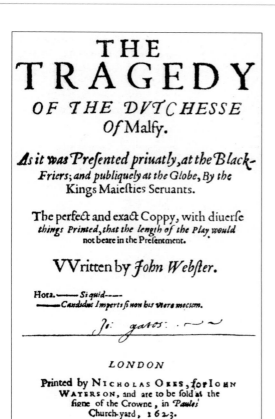

The first printed edition of *The Duchess of Malfi* by John Webster, 1623

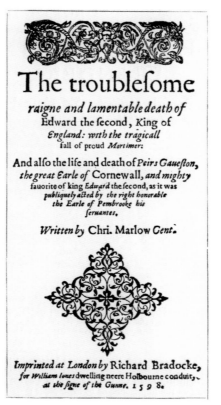

An early edition of *Edward II* by Christopher Marlowe, 1598

Responding to plot innovation

The Jacobeans – Middleton, Webster and Ford – often responded to Elizabethan innovations or traditions by replying to, changing or even mocking an aspect of the plot in those earlier plays. Kyd's plot of his proto-revenge play, *The Spanish Tragedy*, paved the way for every Elizabethan and Jacobean revenge plot that followed. The Jacobeans – Shakespeare's *Hamlet*, *King Lear* and *Macbeth*; the tragedies of Webster, Middleton and Ford – adapted this subgenre with revenge plots that 'spoke back' to Kyd's innovative plot and also reflected the wider social, political and literary contexts of their time.

Intertextual plots

In some cases, *the Jacobean playwrights* adapted or 'replied to' each other in more closely contemporary, Jacobean plays. Middleton (who collaborated with Shakespeare on a few plays) parodies Hamlet's delay (c.1600) in *The Revenger's Tragedy* (c.1606). His rampaging and speedy avenger, Vindice, cries 'hurry, hurry, hurry!' to communicate the sense of urgency that Hamlet lacks in Shakespeare's longest play. This

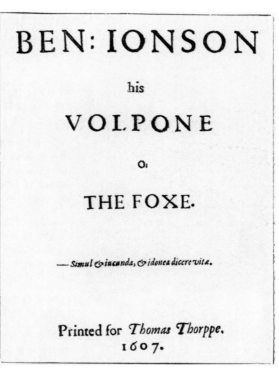

The first printed edition of *Volpone* by Ben Jonson, 1607

Links

For more information, see Chapter 3, 'Biographical contexts': 'Elizabethan and Jacobean intertextuality' (page 19), Chapter 5, 'Tragedy': 'Exploring revenge tragedy' (page 39) and Chapter 12, 'Key influences on tragedy': 'Plot summary' (page 104).

is an example of the intertextuality of the period. A playwright responds to another's plot and storyline, restructuring the action into his own play to challenge or agree with the message or method of their source plot.

If you are studying either of these plays, explore the differences in their revenge plots. Consider how and why they have a differently developed story and narrative structure.

Activity 1

Plots and their sources
Consider your play. Read a summary of the plot and its sources. Answer the following questions.

1. Identify the changes to the storyline and the narrative structure.

2. Identify any differences between the genre (and any subgenres) of your play and the dramatic genre or type of text of the source itself. How are the differences significant for the relationship between plot and context in your play?

3. How have the plot changes influenced your emotional response to the 'new' play or episode? Where do your sympathies now lie? Why? How have the plot changes affected the mood and the outcome of the 'new' play?

4. How does your play use Intertextual references from plots developed in other plays?

5. How does your play use contemporary ideas about the law, gender or social class to drive the plot?

Connections: context, plot, source and genre
Let us consider how the relationships between context, plot, source and genre work in practice.

Activity 2

Connecting plot, genre, source and context
1. Why might Shakespeare write the tragedy of *Macbeth* – the story of a Scottish lord's murderous ambition to become king – just after James I succeeded to the English throne? How is the plot used to reflect Jacobean historical and political contexts of ideas about royal succession?

2. *The Duchess of Malfi* is the story of a young widow who cannot openly marry the man she loves and is killed for her secret choices. The sources (and the story's factual origins) showed no sympathy for her plight. How and why does Webster re-write the plot as a tragedy? How do the source and Webster's plot contrast in their uses of Malfi and the Italian setting?

3. How does Shakespeare parody the conventions of a pastoral comedy and alter his sources for the plot of *As You Like It*? Why?

4. How does Marlowe change his main source, Holinshed's *Chronicles*, to write the individual tragedy of *Edward II*? Why? (You can ask the same question of all the tragic history plays we consider and even *King Lear*.)

Activity 2 (continued)

5. How does Marlowe do the same in his tragedy *Doctor Faustus*? Marlowe's title is *The Tragicall History of the Life and Death of Doctor Faustus* and his source is entitled *The History of the Damnable Life and Deserved Death of Doctor John Faustus*. How has the emphasis shifted?

6. How and why is a tragic plot, such as *Hamlet*, created from a narrative source with no tragic features or supporting cast of revengers?

7. How can the social and political contexts of gender and class be foregrounded to change whose tragedy is being told – for example, in the Jacobean plays: Webster's *The Duchess of Malfi* or *The White Devil*, Middleton's *The Revenger's Tragedy* and Ford's *'Tis Pity She's a Whore*?

8. In *Measure for Measure* and *The Tempest*, two of Shakespeare's tragi-comedies, potential tragedy is averted and the plays end with a comic resolution. How do their plots contribute to these genre outcomes?

Links

For more information, see Chapter 5, 'Defining tragedy' (page 34); 'Pastoral comedies' (page 43); 'Comic resolution and the plot' (page 42).

Beginnings and endings

Let us conclude our investigation into the importance of plot by analysing and comparing the relationships between plot development and the literary context of genre in three plays. The extracts below are from the beginning and ending of each play.

Applying context questions 1

Comparative analysis of plot and genre: beginnings and endings

1. Read the three following extracts. Consider the information you are given, including the dates and stage directions.

2. For each extract, analyse how the playwright uses:

   * the beginning of the play to introduce or suggest how the plot will end

   * the ending of the plot to conclude the play as tragedy, history or comedy.

3. Compare and contrast:

   * how the plot beginnings inform us of the plot outcomes and endings

   * the ways in which the plots are concluded

   * how the plot outcomes contradict or support their beginnings: the relationship between the plot details and the subgenres of each play – that is, what type of tragedy or comedy is in each plot.

4. Apply the analysis to your own play/s. Read 20–50 lines from the beginning and the ending of your texts.

   * Complete question 2 for your play.

   * Complete question 3. Compare your own play with an extract below from the same genre – tragedy, comedy or history.

Extract 1

Christopher Marlowe, *Edward the Second* (1592)

This extract begins and ends the play. Gaveston is the male lover of the king, Edward II. Isabella is Edward's queen. King Edward III is their son. Mortimer Junior is a baron who opposes Edward II and Gaveston and has become the queen's lover.

Scene 1, lines 1–23

Enter GAVESTON *reading on a letter that was brought him from the King.*

GAVESTON
'My father is deceased; come, Gaveston,
And share the kingdom with thy dearest friend.'
Ah, words that make me surfeit with delight!
What greater bliss can hap to Gaveston,
Than live and be the favourite of a king?
Sweet prince, I come; these, thy amorous lines
Might have enforced me to have swum from France,
And, like Leander, gasped upon the sand,
So thou wouldst smile and take me in thy arms.
The sight of London to my exiled eyes
Is as Elysium to a new-come soul;
Not that I love the city or the men,
But that it harbours him I hold so dear,
The King, upon whose bosom let me die,
And with the world be still at enmity.
What need the arctic people love starlight,
To whom the sun shines both by day and night?
Farewell, base stooping to the lordly peers;
My knee shall bow to none but the King.
As for the multitude, that are but sparks
Raked up in embers of their poverty,
Tanti! I'll fan first on the wind
That glanceth at my lips and flieth away.

Scene 25, lines 85–102

KING EDWARD III
Away with her. Her words enforce these tears,
And I shall pity her if she speak again.

ISABELLA
Shall I not mourn for my beloved lord,
And with the rest accompany him to his grave?

SECOND LORD
Thus, madam, 'tis the King's will you shall hence.

ISABELLA
He hath forgotten me; stay, I am his mother.

SECOND LORD
That boots not; therefore, gentle madam, go.

ISABELLA
Then come, sweet death, and rid me of this grief.

[*Exit* ISABELLA, *guarded*]

[*Enter* FIRST LORD *with the head of* MORTIMER JUNIOR]

FIRST LORD
My lord, here is the head of Mortimer.

KING EDWARD III
Go fetch my father's hearse, where it shall lie,
And bring my funeral robes.   [*Exit attendants*]
Accursed head!
Could I have ruled thee then, as I do now,
Thou hadst not hatched this monstrous treachery.

[*Enter attendants with the hearse of
King* EDWARD II *and funeral robes*]

Here comes the hearse; help me to mourn, my lords.
Sweet father, here unto thy murdered ghost
I offer up this wicked traitor's head.
And let these tears, distilling from mine eyes,
Be witness of my grief and innocency.

[*Exeunt, with a funeral march*]

Edward the Second by Christopher Marlowe (1592).
Scene 1, lines 1–23 and Scene 25, lines 85–102

Extract 2

Ben Jonson, *Volpone* (1606)

This extract begins and ends the play. At the start, Volpone (meaning 'the fox') is with his servant, Mosca, who helps him to con people. (They both pretend that Volpone is dying with no one to inherit his wealth. Greedy chancers, already rich, ply him with their wealth, daughters and promises hoping to inherit when he 'soon dies'.) 1st Avocatore is a judge sentencing Volpone at the end. Mosca has been imprisoned.

Act 1, Scene 1, lines 1–27

[*Enter* MOSCA, *pulling back the curtains to discover* VOLPONE *in bed*]

VOLPONE
Good morning to the day; and, next my gold:
Open the shrine, that I may see my saint.

[MOSCA *uncovers the treasure*]

Hail the world's soul, and mine. More glad than is
The teeming earth, to see the longed-for sun
Peep through the horns of the celestial Ram,
Am I, to view thy splendour, darkening his;
That, lying here, amongst my other hoards,
Show'st like a flame by night; or like the day
Struck out of chaos, when all darkness fled
Unto the centre. O thou son of Sol,
But brighter than thy father, let me kiss,
With adoration, thee, and every relic
Of sacred treasure in this blessed room.
Well did wise poets, by thy glorious name,
Title that age which they would have the best,
Thou being the best of things, and far transcending
All style of joy, in children, parents, friends,
Or any other waking dream on earth.
They should have giv'n her twenty thousand Cupids;
Such are thy beauties, and our loves! Dear saint,
Riches, the dumb god that giv'st all men tongues;
That canst do nought, and yet mak'st men do all things;
The price of souls; even hell, with thee to boot,
Is made worth heaven! Thou art virtue, fame,
Honour, and all things else! Who can get thee,
He shall be noble, valiant, honest, wise –

Act 5, Scene 12, lines 116–125

1st AVOCATORE
Thou, Volpone,
By blood and rank a gentleman, canst not fall
Under like censure; but our judgement on thee
Is, that thy substance all be straight confiscate
To the hospital of the *Incurabili*;
And, since the most was gotten by imposture,
By feigning lame, gout, palsy and such diseases,
Thou art to lie in prison, cramped with irons,
Till thou be'st sick and lame indeed. Remove him.

VOLPONE
This is called mortifying of a fox.

Epilogue, lines 1–6

[*Enter* VOLPONE *as* EPILOGUE]

The seasoning of a play is the applause.
Now, though the fox be punished by the laws,
He yet doth hope there is no suff'ring due
For any fact which he hath done 'gainst you.
If there be, censure him; here he doubtful stands.
If not, fare jovially, and clap your hands.

THE END

Volpone by Ben Jonson (1606). Act 1, Scene 1, lines 1–27,
Act 5, Scene 12, lines 116–125 and Epilogue, lines 1–6

Extract 3

William Shakespeare, *Macbeth* (1606)

This extract begins with an early scene where the Witches go on the heath to find Macbeth, a thane (Scottish lord), and fortell his destiny – to become the Thane of Cawdor then King of Scotland. Banquo (another thane) is prophesised by the Witches to be the father of kings. (When the play begins, the King of Scotland is Duncan. Obsessed with this prophesy, Macbeth kills him that night, becomes king and later kills Banquo, who visits Macbeth as a ghost. Battles ensue.) The extract finishes with the end of the play, after Macduff, a thane loyal to Malcolm, has killed Macbeth. Malcolm (Duncan's son) is now the King of Scotland.

Act 1, Scene 3, lines 45–59

MACBETH
Speak if you can: what are you?

FIRST WITCH
All hail Macbeth, hail to thee, Thane of Glamis.

SECOND WITCH
All hail Macbeth, hail to thee, Thane of Cawdor.

THIRD WITCH
All hail Macbeth, that shalt be king hereafter.

BANQUO
Good sir, why do you start and seem to fear
Things that do sound so fair? – I'th'name of truth
Are ye fantastical, or that indeed
Which outwardly ye show? My noble partner
You greet with present grace and great prediction
Of noble having and of royal hope
That he seems rapt withal. To me you speak not.
If you can look into the seeds of time
And say which grain will grow and which will not,
Speak then to me, who neither beg nor fear
Your favours nor your hate.

Act 5, Scene 9, lines 21–42

Enter MACDUFF, *with Macbeth's head*
MACDUFF
Hail, king, for so thou art. Behold where stands
Th'usurper's cursed head. The time is free.
I see thee compassed with thy kingdom's pearl,
That speak my salutation in their minds;
Whose voices I desire aloud with mine.
Hail, King of Scotland.
ALL   Hail, King of Scotland.
Flourish

MALCOLM
We shall not spend a large expense of time
Before we reckon with your several loves
And make us even with you. My thanes and kinsmen,
Henceforth be earls, the first that ever Scotland
In such an honour named. What's more to do
Which would be planted newly with the time, –
As calling home our exiled friends abroad
That fled the snares of watchful tyranny,
Producing forth the cruel ministers
Of this dead butcher and his fiend-like queen,
Who, as 'tis thought, by self and violent hands
Took off her life, – this and what needful else
That calls upon us, by the grace of Grace
We will perform measure in measure, time, and place.
So, thanks to all at once and to each one,
Whom we invite to see us crowned at Scone.
Flourish
Exeunt

FINIS

Macbeth by William Shakespeare (1606). Act 1, Scene 3, lines 45–59 and Act 5, Scene 9, lines 21–42

Summary

This chapter has introduced you to how plots were constructed in Elizabethan and Jacobean drama. You have considered some significant relationships between plot and context:

- the use of sources
- plot and dramatic genres
- connections between context, plot, source and genre
- the dramatic significance for the beginnings and endings of drama from this period.

7   Themes

Defining 'theme'

As you know plot is more than the story; dramatic plot is the way in which the narrative structure and the ideas of the dramatist are shared with the audience. Within a plot, the dramatist frames the ideas and concepts. These develop as themes, along with the events of the story and the fortunes of the characters, and are concluded – gravely, happily or uncertainly – as the play ends.

The importance of theme

The importance of theme can be answered with another question: when the stories are over, what remains? Beyond the plot or the characters in a play, a 21st-century audience may still think, act and feel in many of the same ways as the original audience. This common experience is part of our human condition – particularly some of the inescapable aspects of our condition, like death or loss – and goes beyond context. You will find that some of the themes in your play, Elizabethan or Jacobean, will be recognisable to you because of this shared humanity.

Universal themes

Themes deal with the big questions in life that can transcend time or place – be it Elizabethan, Jacobean, England, or your own time/place. Themes can give drama a universal element. This is especially true of Shakespeare's plays and some by Marlowe. You can also see a 21st-century British theatre revival of Jacobean tragedies by Webster, Middleton and Ford.

Perhaps we engage with the questions of the play to find our own answers. We might disagree with how ideas are aired or concluded, possibly because of our differing contexts. No answers may be offered, either by us or the play itself. Being part of the questioning might be enough for us: to know that we are not alone in our experiences and ideas.

Themes in context

There might be differences between how Elizabethan and Jacobean audiences interpreted themes or ideas and how you understand and interpret them today. For example, differences in:

- the dramatic treatment of ideas (literary contexts)
- the impact of those ideas on the different audiences (contexts of reception)
- the ways in which each society manages its thoughts, feelings and belief systems around those ideas (the historical, political, social and cultural contexts).

These differences stem from contexts of the period, theirs and yours. Let us consider the significant themes you could find in your plays and what is specifically Elizabethan or Jacobean about their treatment.

Chapter aims

In this chapter we will focus on the relationship between theme and context in Elizabethan and Jacobean drama. We will explore:

- a definition of 'theme'
- significant themes in context
- an analysis of the relationship between theme and context in your drama text.

Did you know?

Identifying themes
You can spot a theme by its name – ask the question: what is the play about? If the answer is a description of events and characters, that is the storyline in the plot. If the answer is a list of abstract nouns about human qualities or experiences, such as 'love' or 'kingship', these are the themes.

Remember

Universal themes
The universal themes contribute to why people want to watch or study a play hundreds of years later as the ideas behind the plot still feel relevant or important to us today.

Examiner's tip

Theme and context
Do not state the obvious. For example: all tragedy is about death, or all romantic comedy is about marriage.

Do be specific. For example: how do particular themes reveal particular contexts in your plays?

Links

Use Chapters 4 and 5 (pages 21–32 and 33–44) to help you to understand themes in the contexts of your drama.

Hieronimo and Bel-Imperia grieve for the murdered Horatio in Thomas Kyd's *The Spanish Tragedy*

Significant themes in context

These are as follows:

- Death
- Love, sex and lust
- Behaviour codes
- Disguise and concealment.
- Power

Death

Death through illness or old age rarely has thematic significance in your play. Death is not dramatised as part of ordinary life in Elizabethan and Jacobean drama. Let us focus on how death is explored as a dramatic theme, according to genre.

History

In a history play, ideas about death serve the plot-line of succession to the throne. A king or heir dies or inherits when their ancestor dies. Death is presented as part of the inevitability of that system. The tragic history is more interesting on death and can be considered with tragedy later in this chapter.

Comedy

As we know, characters in an Elizabethan or Jacobean comedy do not die, either as punishment or as victims of any villainy and treachery in the play. In comedy, death has a different role to play:

- Some comic plots introduce or interweave a previous death, a back story from before the play begins. The comic resolution at the end can provide a healing of past problems, as well as a solution to the present problems.

- The back story to a prior death can be tied to money, wealth and inheritance. These deaths might be presented thematically as issues of justice as part of the comic resolution. This kind of death can also be presented as a source of resentment or injustice. For example, in *As You Like It*, Orlando resents how his brother Jacques was favoured in his father's will, now dead and unchangeable. The comic ending resolves the theme of death and resentment.

- Death can have satirical overtones. For example, in *Volpone*, death is presented thematically through the pretence of Volpone's impending 'death' within ideas on deceitfulness and greed.

- Death is not a source of sadness in a comedy. Death can be presented thematically as a *potential* cause of loss and grieving. For example, in *Twelfth Night*, we have Viola and her missing, ship-wrecked brother Sebastian, presumed drowned. The comic resolution means that he is found and becomes happily married, along with his sister who temporarily grieved for him. Death here is a source of dramatic tension and even dramatic irony once the audience knows that Sebastian, the 'dead' brother, is alive. His 'return from the dead' and the fact that he is identical to his sister implicate him in various tangled love-plots. The theme of imagined death has a comic impact on the audience here.

Tragi-comedy

- Shakespeare wrote tragi-comedies. Many of the points above, in 'Comedy', are relevant here but many of the points in 'Tragedy' (below) also apply.

- The threat of death can cast an ominous shadow over comic plots but it does not last. Any danger of death will be averted either by a main character or by the plot-line of an 'accident' or solution. If you are studying *Measure for Measure* or *The Tempest,* consider whether the threat and danger of death is lifted permanently from the characters. Does anyone die in sacrifice to the comic plot? None of the central characters meet that end in tragi-comedy.

Tragedy

Death is an essential theme in the tragedy genre. The heroes and protagonists of a tragedy or tragic history will all die. The questions to ask of a tragedy are: who dies, when, how and why? Death usually occurs through murder, sometimes suicide, often as an act of revenge or to dispense some other sort of justice.

Accidental death can be part of the maelstrom of tragic deaths, in which the wrong person is killed by mistake. Accidental death in Elizabethan and Jacobean tragedy is still rooted in intentions to murder. Characters who die accidentally in your plays do not die in 'an accident' – such as falling off a ladder – but because they take the fatally wrong action or are in the fatally wrong place when the planned murder is enacted. For example, in *The Revenger's Tragedy*, the wrong brother is executed because of a mix-up in their imprisonment, and in *Hamlet*, Polonius and Gertrude die as a result of the mistaken actions or murderous plans of Hamlet and Claudius respectively.

Murder

Murder is presented as an act of brutality; often bloody, frenzied and graphically described or acted. Through the act of murder, death is presented as a thematic symbol of violence or treachery. Where there is an accomplice, the theme of death may be linked to ideas about motivation for murder. For example, Macbeth and Lady Macbeth's plot to murder King Duncan, or Ambitioso and Supervacuo's plot to have their eldest brother executed in *The Revenger's Tragedy*.

Where secrecy is required to protect the identity of the murderer, the dramatist might use the method of poison or a concealed weapon. For example, Claudius's several murders in *Hamlet* or Brachiano's murder of his wife in *The White Devil*. A secret murder presents the thematic relationship between death and deceit. This might link themes of death and corruption in your play.

Where the murderer is presented as dastardly rather than noble, the method of death might reflect that. In this period, a sword duel is more focused on themes of honour than death. Presentations of murder in your plays are not dignified by a respectable sword duel. Daggers might be used for these deaths. The murder could be particularly gruesome, debauched or blood-thirsty. For example, Giovanni tearing out his sister's heart in *'Tis Pity She's a Whore*, or the sadistic use of a poker in *Edward II*. In this case, murder is being presented as unacceptable or unjust, linking the theme of murder to justice and honour.

Revenge

In revenge tragedy, the act of revenge is presented as compulsory within themes of justice and honour. Each of the revenge tragedies (or plays with elements, acts or threats of revenge) explores ideas of revenge in the context of their own society.

Think about it

Suicide, madness and honour

The dramatist might use the act of suicide to develop other themes such as madness or honour. What does the relationship between suicide, madness and honour reveal about the social, cultural and literary contexts in Elizabethan and Jacobean drama? If there is an act of suicide in your play/s, how does its presentation show you the contexts of your text?

Did you know?

The symbolism of violence

In Elizabethan and Jacobean tragedy, the act of removing or violating a body part originates from Greek and Roman tragedy and is used to symbolise a theme in the play and its presentation in the maimed character. For example:

- cutting out a heart symbolises absence or loss of love

- plucking out eyes symbolises inability to see and a lack of awareness

- strangulation/suffocation/cutting or biting out a tongue symbolises having no voice or being silenced

- anal insertion of a red-hot poker symbolises rape, powerlessness, the stripping of masculinity, position and status.

In *The Spanish Tragedy* the theme of revenge has a straightforward presentation: it is righteous and the only course of action. Revenge is presented in the contexts of a social and cultural ritual and the avenger simply carries out his role.

As you know, there are genre developments and deviations even within the subgenre of revenge tragedy. Revenge can appear to be a gratifying, even pleasurable, act for the avenger. Your play could present revenge as burdensome, as in *Hamlet*, or mock the seriousness of contemplating and enacting revenge, like *The Revenger's Tragedy*. Your play might question the morality of revenge, as in *The Duchess of Malfi* through the Duchess's Machiavellian brothers, and in *The White Devil* through the corrupt Duke. Webster presents these avengers as dishonourable, lascivious and unjust in their actions and motivations. Some later Jacobean plays make the revenge acts so diabolical that they seem to parody the revenge theme itself, such as *'Tis Pity She's a Whore*.

Justice

The relationship between themes of justice and death by murder and revenge is complex in Elizabethan and Jacobean drama. Both the social contexts and the context of reception will dominate the audience's response to whether the death is justified, then and now. Elizabethan murders might be set against the Christian ethos of paying for your sins. For example, Marlowe debates this presentation of death and justice in *Doctor Faustus*. Death might be presented as a divine or evil punishment and therefore just – in the themes of the play and the eyes of the contemporary audience.

Avengers might be presented with their idea of a revenge code as the only justice: of swiftly avenging a death of a family member or kinsman. You might feel that rough justice is dispensed in the drama of this period. Conversely, you might feel that the death is entirely just, even if tragic or simply sad, or you might feel horrified at the unjust nature of the death. For example, the murder of the Duchess of Malfi's children or Lady Macduff's in *Macbeth*. Your plays often use the theme of justice to debate ideas about the necessity of death.

> ### Think about it
>
> **Rights and wrongs of revenge**
>
> How does the approach to revenge in your play/s reveal the contexts that influenced the playwright/s?

> ### Link
>
> For more information, see Chapter 4, 'Contexts of revenge for the Elizabethans' (page 22).

> ### Think about it
>
> **Law and punishment in your drama**
>
> Consider the following questions. In your play:
>
> - Who avoids full punishment under the law?
> - Who escapes punishment entirely?
> - Who gets justice from the law?
> - Who benefits, or not, from the law of state-dispensed punishment?
> - How do these presentations of law and punishment reveal Elizabethan and Jacobean ideas about the 'right and wrong' behaviour or treatment of people?

> ### Activity 1
>
> **The theme of death**
> Consider the deaths in your plays.
>
> - Who dies? When? How? Why?
> - How does the presentation of death in your play/s demonstrate the significance of Elizabethan and Jacobean contexts?

Behaviour codes
The law and punishment

As you know, private and personal justice by revenge became illegal during the Elizabethan era. By the time your plays were written, a single state law had replaced the vigilante revenge code.

In practice, this law and the punishment dispensed in Elizabethan and Jacobean England operated according to your social status. It was easier to escape harsh punishment with royal favour and influence. The punishment for treason was famously to be hanged, drawn and quartered – unless you were from the nobility, and then you only lost your head. Does your play have any examples of this differentiated practice of the law and punishment for acts of murder and revenge?

However, there was a new understanding that individual murderers could not legally rampage around the country or city, plotting and killing their enemies without consequences from the state. Despite this, there remained some sympathy with the old order of settling disputes yourself. Coupled with the growing Jacobean unrest with the monarchy, the law could be held in low regard. How does your drama explore ways in which the law is viewed in the society of the play? Is the thematic presentation of the law in your play concerned with punishment of crimes other than murder?

> ## Did you know?
>
> **Jacobean playwrights and lawyers**
> Middleton, Webster and Ford practised law at one of the Inns of Court in London. You might notice or research that their dramatic language often has styles and structures of a legal argument, especially Ford's.

The Duke and Escalus, attended by the provost, dispense justice at the end of *Measure For Measure*

Honour

The theme of honour is linked with power and kingship on the following pages. For an Elizabethan or Jacobean, honour meant family and personal honour, as it does in many cultures today. Revenge killings to protect your honour remained a part of this philosophy. Marriage was equally significant in matters of honour. Protecting your honour was vital to social status, family position and personal – usually male – pride. Protecting honour extended to property as well as people. Women were legal property and this was reflected in social attitudes. Courage and strength was for men, virtue and obedience was for women – this was honour. Honourable behaviour, including vengeance when one's honour was compromised, reflected this contemporary belief. How is the theme of honour – individual, family, national or royal – presented in your drama?

> ## Activity 2
>
> **Justice, law, punishment and honour in context**
> Consider the presentation of the themes of justice, law, punishment and honour in your plays. What do they tell you about the legal and social position of women, the poor, the Church, the king, lords and barons at the time the drama was written?

> ## Links
>
> For more information, see Chapter 2, 'The macro contexts': 'Political backgrounds' (page 10); 'Social contexts' (page 11).

The Wheel of Fortune

Many Elizabethans and Jacobeans held the older medieval belief that life moved in a circle from birth to death, represented visually as a wheel controlled by Lady Fortune. The height of your fortune was at the top of the wheel, the bottom was the result of a fall. The wheel spun and you went up or down but never knew if it would spin again for you.

The balance of power

The theme of power in a play can be expressed through the dramatic structure. A shift in power, political or personal, can be explored through a shift in setting or mood. A scene change can alert the audience to thematic changes in where the power lies.

Think about it

Powerful women in context

A powerful woman – like Lady Macbeth, Cordelia in *King Lear* or Webster's Duchess – shows how the dramatist presents a gender shift in the power-balance **within** the play – even if that shift in power does not last beyond their death. How might this reflect a challenge of ideas about power-balance in the social order outside of the play?

Remember

Presentations of greed

Greed is a significant theme in some plays from this period and links with power, lust and envy. Presentations and criticisms of greed are particularly important in *Volpone* and *Doctor Faustus*. These plays can be compared for their focus on the title characters' endless materialistic desires.

Power

Power is defined by political and social status. The theme of power is presented in cycles in your drama. You could have your hands on power at one moment but that might be destroyed if you lacked vigilance. It was vital to maintain and protect your power interests, especially for a ruling monarch.

The theme of power might be presented through an individual or a group relationship. Look for power shifts between characters in couples and families. Ideas about power-balance in your plays might appear to challenge the contemporary social norms. Sometimes they serve to reinforce the contemporary social and political power hierarchy.

Activity 3

Mapping power in your play

1. Identify who has power in your play. Decide what kind of power it is. (For example, a king has political power and absolute power.) Consider who has the most and the least power and create a hierarchy of power for the characters in your play.

2. Think about the 'Wheel of Fortune' and the 'balance of power'. Explore if and how power changes hands, temporarily or permanently.

3. Compare the beginning with the ending: consider if and how the power has shifted and the significance of the shift.

Kingship and rule

The political and military machinations of powerful rulers are key themes in histories of all types and some tragedies. The subgenre of the individual tragedy is a thematic struggle for power between those who have it and those who want it, the one losing it and the one who thinks he deserves it. For example, the power struggles in *Richard II*.

Order and disorder

The themes of order and disorder can work at both political and personal levels in your plays. At a social and political level, the play might be concerned with presentations of:

- preservation or destruction of regimes and traditions: such as the reassertion of control by the royal court in Athens at the end of *A Midsummer Night's Dream*, or the toppling of a dynasty with Vindice's murder of the Duke in *The Revenger's Tragedy*

- the movement from an old order to a new order, possibly religious: such as the movement towards Protestantism and beliefs in humanism explored in *Doctor Faustus*

- the dabbling or tampering by someone in power, like Edward II or King Lear – or even someone who is not – who disrupts the social order in the play.

The theme of disruption is present in both comedy and tragedy and can be executed by the powerful and the powerless characters in the play. Comic examples include Puck and the fairies interfering in the human love and power struggles in *A Midsummer Night's Dream*, and Viola's cross-dressing which causes havoc in *Twelfth Night*. Tragic examples are: Flamineo causing disorder when he manipulates the lives of both his own lower-status family and Brachiano the Duke in Webster's *The White Devil*; the Witches in *Macbeth* who are used to prophesy the disorder that Macbeth and Lady Macbeth go on to create.

Themes of order and disorder could be presented on a personal level, affecting individuals rather than the whole of society in your plays. However, if the individual is powerful – a ruler or someone with high social status – their personal engagement with order and disorder affects the workings of society in the play. For example: the social and moral disorder of King Claudius's corruption is presented as corrupting the whole state of Denmark; Prince Hamlet's engagement with madness, whether feigned or genuine, disrupts the entire society of the royal house of Denmark and the chances of harmony in the state.

Chaos and madness

The theme of chaos is presented as part of disorder in your drama. Chaos can be presented in personal ways through an individual's dysfunctional behaviour or at a social and political level through the collapse of social order and the established ruling hierarchy. In *'Tis Pity She's a Whore*, Giovanni is disturbed by the frustrations and effects of his incestuous love and desire, which cause chaos, and his actions devastate his family. Ferdinand, the twin brother of the Duchess of Malfi, contributes to the chaos of the palace and its wider society through his incestuous desire for his widowed sister and his refusal of her remarriage.

Ideas about madness are often presented to show how an individual is driven insane by their actions and contemplations, especially if corrupt moral values are operating on the world of the play, either through the avenger himself or those on whom he seeks revenge.

Presentations of madness feature:

- a feeble or frail descent into chaos
- an empowering disguise or release
- a consequence of immoral thoughts and behaviour
- a tragic response to an overwhelming, traumatic situation.

Vindice, holding his wife's skull, in *The Revenger's Tragedy*

Remember

Madness in context
The disturbed mind is a significant theme in the tragedy of this period. It reveals contemporary ideas about political and personal corruption and the Elizabethan and Jacobean appetite for the stories and dramatic subgenre of revenge tragedy.

Activity 4

Madness in your play
Shakespeare tells us that 'Madness in great ones must not unwatched go' (*Hamlet* Act 3, Scene 1, line 189). This line is spoken by King Claudius and refers to Prince Hamlet. Claudius has secretly poisoned his elder brother (Hamlet's father) and married the Queen (Hamlet's mother). He has robbed Hamlet of his family and his throne and is worried that Hamlet suspects.

1. How do you think Shakespeare uses ideas about madness in this line? Consider the contexts and the information above on the plot and the characters.

2. How does your play use ideas about madness or disruption? Consider the relationship between the theme and the contexts of the play.

Love, sex and lust

Love

Things were not as grim as the tragedies suggest. They still had love. A romantic comedy debates ideas on love and ends in marriage between everyone involved in that debate, usually happily for both parties – but not always. For example, in *As You Like It*, Touchstone and Audrey marry but the prognosis for happiness is not good. Tragi-comedies present love as rescued from the jaws of death and tragedy and end in a similar way to romantic comedy. For example, Claudio and Juliet in *Measure for Measure*. However, love is sometimes presented as doomed. Not everyone gets their heart's desire in Elizabethan and Jacobean drama. For example, Ophelia does not marry Hamlet, or even survive the tragic events of the play.

The theme of love in a tragedy, even where the love story is the plot and the characters are lovers, is a doomed and tragic affair – the tragic hero's hamartia may be his love for someone, such as Antony's for Cleopatra. In *The Duchess of Malfi* and *'Tis Pity She's a Whore*, the tragedy of forbidden love is hers. Tragedy from this period shows the audience that love has no power to rescue the protagonists from the tragic ending.

In your play/s, parental love is often manifested in themes of power, ownership and inheritance or jealousy and abandonment. Ideas on ownership and manipulation, especially of daughters and sisters, tend to be foregrounded. Examples include the pimping of Castiza in *The Revenger's Tragedy* and of Vittoria in *The White Devil*. In *King Lear*, Gloucester is presented as an untypical example of a loving father (although his bastard son presents a different view). He is a foil to Lear and his unhappy relationships with his daughters. Parental love is rarely a nurturing theme of maternal and paternal care, even in comedy.

Sex and lust

Thematically, sex treads a precarious path in your plays. It is acceptable as the butt of jokes, expected from bawdy and vulgar characters, natural in young and beautiful lovers and the joyful reward of a sanctified marriage between lovers of the same social class and the opposite gender. Otherwise, it is classed as lust and treated as a sin.

In romantic comedy of this period, sex is presented as ordinary and sociable – after you were married. In a satire or city comedy it is presented as seedy and exploitative. In a tragedy, it is the root of some evil and its pleasure is fleeting. Sex in a tragedy can be linked to the demise of those involved. It often signifies corruption of the society and the soul, especially when it is practised by siblings or high-ranking church officials. In a tragi-comedy, it could be any of the above. In a history it is for the begetting of kings, in a tragic history it usually ends in execution. The thematic significance of sex and desire is embedded in the narrative structure of the play and often drives the plot: who is doing it, with whom, why and its consequences in the drama are the important questions to ask when you analyse the relationship between theme and context in your play.

Disguise and concealment

Love in disguise

Themes of love and sex either depend on or contribute to themes of mistakes and disguises. Plot devices such as mistaken identity and

> **Think about it**
>
> **Sex in context**
> Ambivalent ideas about sex are presented in drama from this period. Why? How do the contexts influence presentations of sexual feelings and relationships in your plays?

misinformation about who loved whom – deliberate or unwitting – and ideas about deceit and duplicity are used to further or halt a love story or sexual encounter in the comedy and tragedy of this period. The thematic relationship of love and disguise is especially true of comedy and tragi-comedy. If you are studying either of these genres, consider how disguise is important for the love story in the plot.

Death in disguise

The theme of death, particularly murder and revenge, can be linked to the theme of concealment in tragedy of this period. Disguise is presented as physical and emotional. The presentation of avengers or murderers who hide their identity or/and their feelings can be used to intensify dramatic tension and create dramatic irony. The theme of disguise can also be used to escape an anticipated punishment or murder and present feelings of fear and self-preservation.

All the plays we consider use ideas about disguise and concealment to explore themes of love or death. Whichever genre or concealed character you consider, the disguise is fundamental to the intricate plotting and narrative structure of the drama. Consider your play/s:

- How is disguise used in the plot to explore the themes of love or/and death?
- How does the presentation of disguise engage your emotional response to aspects of the play?
- How far does the disguise depend on the use of dramatic irony?
- How does the use of disguise affect the relationship between the audience and the concealed characters?

Analysis of theme and context in your drama text

Applying context questions 1

The dramatic presentation of themes of love and sex in context

Read the two extracts below from different types of play and the background information.

1. For each extract, analyse how the dramatist uses the theme of sexual love to explore:

   - the social taboos that are debated or avoided
   - the social complications of relationships in the play.

2. Consider your own plays. Select an extract of 20–50 lines which explores the theme of sexual love and wooing.
   Analyse how your extract explores the theme of sexual love in the contexts of your play, both macro and literary.

3. Compare and contrast how you respond to the presentations of sexual love across the extracts.
   Analyse how the context of reception influences your responses.

Examiner's tip

The language of themes in context

AO2 is the use of language, form and structure in your plays. Make sure you consider how the extract or play has been constructed to communicate themes or ideas. Consider how the contexts influence the dramatic language.

Background information for the task

Note: the exact dates of composition of these two plays are not known – the dates given below cover the likely period of writing.

- **Genre**

  The first extract is from an Elizabethan romantic comedy, a cross-dressing tale of love, desire and disguise. The second is a Jacobean revenge tragedy, with themes that are so extreme they parody the subgenre.

- **Situation, or context, within the play**

  Both extracts feature a dialogue between a wooer and the object of their desire. In each scene the pair is alone and the aim is for one to gain sexual love from the other. Each involves a taboo.

- **Plot**

  In the first extract, Lady Olivia woos a young man, Cesario, who is not only a servant (on a mission to woo her for his master) but also a secretly disguised woman, Viola. Ironically, Olivia has summoned 'Cesario' under false pretences, unaware that the bigger falseness is 'Cesario's' disguise. No romance develops from this scenario. At the end of the play, Olivia marries Viola's identical twin brother.

In the second extract, the man, Giovanni, against the advice of his friar, woos a woman whom he knows is his sister, Annabella. She is also being courted by several 'suitable' suitors. After this scene, they have sex in secret. Annabella later marries one of the suitors and rejects Giovanni, who kills her at the end.

Extract 1

VIOLA
Madam, I come to whet your gentle thoughts
On his behalf.

OLIVIA   O by your leave, I pray you!
I bade you never again speak of him;
But would you undertake another suit
I had rather hear you to solicit that,
Than music from the spheres.

VIOLA   Dear Lady –

OLIVIA
Give me leave, beseech you, I did send,
After the last enchantment you did here,

A ring in chase of you. So did I abuse
Myself, my servant, and, I fear me, you.
Under your hard construction must I sit,
To force that on you in a shameful cunning
Which you knew none of yours. What might you think?
Have you not set mine honour at the stake,
And baited it with all th'unmuzzled thoughts
That tyrannous heart can think? To one of your receiving
Enough is shown; a cypress, not a bosom,
Hides my heart: so, let me hear you speak.

VIOLA
I pity you.

Twelfth Night by William Shakespeare
(1600–1601). Act 3, Scene 1, lines 90–108

Extract 2

ANABELLA
You are my brother, Giovanni.

GIOVANNI   You
My sister, Anabella. I know this,
And could afford you instance why to love
So much the more for this, to which intent
Wise Nature first in your creation meant
To make you mine; else't had been sin and foul
To share one beauty to a double soul.
Nearness in birth or blood doth but persuade
A nearer nearness in affection.
I have asked counsel of the holy Church,
Who tells me I may love you; and 'tis just
That, since I may, I should; and will, yes will.
Must I now live, or die?

ANABELLA   Live. Thou hast won
The field, and never fought: what thou hast urged,
My captive heart had long ago resolved.
I blush to tell thee (but I'll tell thee now),
For every sigh that thou hast spent for me,
I have sighed ten; for every tear shed twenty;
And not so much that I loved, as that
I durst not say I loved, nor scarcely think it.

GIOVANNI
Let not this music be a dream, ye gods, For pity's
sake I beg 'ee!

'Tis Pity She's a Whore by John Ford
(1629–1633). Act 1, Scene 2, lines 227–248

Summary

In this chapter you have developed your understanding of how themes in Elizabethan and Jacobean drama have been constructed in context. You have explored:

- a definition of theme
- significant themes in context
- how to analyse themes in texts and contexts.

8 Characters

Chapter aims

In this chapter we focus on the significance of the relationship between context and character in Elizabethan and Jacobean drama. We will explore:

- a definition of 'characterisation'
- how to analyse character
- significant character types in context
- how to analyse the relationship between context and character in your drama text.

Links

For more information, see Chapter 5, 'Tragedy': 'Aristotle and the Greeks' (page 34), Chapter 3, 'The genre': 'The "realisable" text' (page 14).

Remember

Extent of the construct

Even when the dramatist constructs for the character/s a complex personality and a psychological profile, the character is still a dramatic construct and not a real person. Even if the drama is based on real events and people, once their characters have been dramatised they become dramatic constructs and are no longer independent of the drama.

Defining 'characterisation'

Believable characters

The fact that you can find a character believable as a potential, 'real person' does not affect the importance of characterisation in your play. Elizabethan and Jacobean dramatists knew that for you to be interested in the fortunes of the characters they had to make them convincing and credible or you would not care what happens to them. In tragedy, it is vital that you care. In comedy, it is important that you remain curious as to how it all ends.

What is 'real'?

The idea that the text can be made 'real' through performance is about the nature of drama. Drama is the **acted** text in which speech and action on a **stage resembles** real speech and action. The importance of acting, resemblance and stage is vital here. It reminds you that you are watching something that has been written even though it might appear that it is actually happening to the people you are watching.

Construct and context

It is difficult to analyse your character types and explore their characterisation in context if you pursue the 'real person' approach to why a character has said or done something. There is only one reason that a character does or says anything – because that is what the dramatist wanted from their role or construct in the play. All that a character says is relevant to their characterisation. Their presence or absence on stage is deliberate. Their actions and relationships are by design. However complicated or simple the speech, actions and relationships of a character, it is constructed to reveal whatever ideas and themes the dramatist is trying to show you as the plot develops. Consequently, all characters and their characterisations are created in both the contexts of the play itself and the contexts of the period – in your case, the Elizabethan and Jacobean period.

How to analyse character

Analysis of your characters, their characterisation and dramatic functions in the play informs you about the contexts operating within your drama. You can begin by exploring characterisation in Activity 1 below.

The dramatic function of characters

Activity 1 has shown you how to observe and question the ways in which character is constructed: where, when and how a character appears in the play. The presentation of characters in the play can tell you more than you might have identified in your log above. Characters have a dramatic function: **why** they are in the play. A consideration of the dramatic function of the characters in your play is essential to complete your analysis of characterisation.

Activity 1

Analysing character
To analyse character construction in your plays, start a log or table of your characters.

1. **Either** observe one character at a time in the order of his or her appearances in the play **or** look at all the characters in a scene or act. Each method is useful for your analysis.

2. Make notes on the bullet points below for each character. Note when, where and with whom they appear, including silent appearances. (From this you will gain an overview of your character's stage presence and absence in the play to use later.)

   - Speech: style (for example, monologue, dialogue, soliloquy, aside), tone/mood, significant silences/pauses

   - Actions: what they do, plan and think (their attitudes and behaviour)

   - Relationships with other characters

   - Views on other characters and what other characters say about them

   - Character type (you can use the list of examples in the next section)

   - Position and role within the power hierarchy of the play

   - Shifts in attitude, behaviour, relationships and position in the play – their character development.

One function is to entertain, inform or instruct the audience in whatever aspects of the plot the character engages. An important dramatic function of a character is to represent particular ideas, themes and symbols that the dramatist explores and communicates to you in the play. Some characters have a greater dramatic importance than others. This is not always reflected by how often they are on stage or how much they say (although you will have all this information about them from completing Activity 1) but in their importance in the **structure** of the play. Activity 2 shows you how to undertake an analysis of the dramatic function of your characters.

Activity 2

Character and dramatic function
Identify the character you want to analyse. Use the information in your log from Activity 1. Consider the dramatic function of the character. Explore how your character contributes to:

- the plot or any subplots – narrative significance

- stage presence, silence and absence – significance in the direction/influence of events/other characters

- ideas or themes of the play, including the development of other characters – their thematic significance

- The structure of the play – their structural significance

- the genre of the play – their tragic or comic significance (you can use the section on 'Character type and genre' below).

Examiner's tip

Understanding characterisation
Try to begin your sentence or point with 'The dramatist [or his/her name] tells us ...' This shows that you understand characterisation because you know that the dramatist – and not the character – constructs the plot and themes of the play.

Common pitfalls
Avoid beginning your sentence or point with 'Hamlet [or a character's name] is ...' This is an example that might lead you to describe a character and their actions or summarise the plot. It will lead you away from analysis and the significance of your characters in the context of the play.

Link

For more information, see Chapter 9, 'Dramatic techniques' (page 81).

Remember

Catalysts
A character that is also a catalyst is given a significant part in the direction of the plot – something happens or is averted in the play as a result of their actions or speech. This, in turn, has an impact upon the development of the themes of the play.

Links

For more information, see Chapter 5, 'Literary contexts' (pages 33–44) and Chapter 7, 'Themes' (pages 53–63).

Links

For more information, see Chapter 5, 'Tragedy': 'The tragic hero' (page 34) and 'The tragedy of the individual' (page 36), Chapter 6, 'Plot and dramatic genres' (page 46) and Chapter 7, 'Significant themes in context' (page 54).

Links

For more information, see Chapter 3, 'Literary contexts': 'The subgenres' (page 14) and Chapter 5, 'Tragedy': 'What the Romans did for us' (page 37).

Think about it

Character type and macro contexts
Consider the cast list from your play. Compare it with those from Kyd and the *commedia dell'arte* in Chapter 12. Try to consider some other Elizabethan and Jacobean plays. Compile a list of character types that occur across the dramas. Use the list of character types to guide you or to compare with afterwards.

Activities 1 and 2 have given you a sound analysis of your character/s and their dramatic functions. You can also consider the ways in which context is significant in the construction and dramatic functions of your characters.

Significant character types in context
Character type and genre

Some character types in Elizabethan and Jacobean drama are tied to a genre, for example, the tragic hero. There are many character types who appear across the genres. For example, the clergy, the aristocracy, the working class, the villain, the clown and the malcontent.

Some character types are taken from earlier styles and subgenres of drama, such as medieval morality plays. For example, morality figures of angels and devils or The Seven Deadly Sins. Other types are taken from the subgenre of Senecan revenge tragedy. For example, a representation of human qualities and motivations, such as the figure of Revenge who appears in Kyd's *The Spanish Tragedy*. Some character types are not tied to a genre or a subgenre but are specific theatrical constructions, such as the malcontent.

Character type and macro contexts

The malcontent in drama from this period is also an example of a character type that is dependent on social and political roles that existed in the contexts of an Elizabethan or Jacobean English society. Additionally, your dramatist might have created the character type for the society within the play, perhaps from an earlier historical period or from outside England. For example, the ways in which the characters of the king, the baron, the duke or the fool have been constructed. Some are not even presentations of human beings. For example, ghosts and fairies.

Character types in your plays

Let us explore the character types that you are likely to find in your plays:

- rulers
- heroes and villains
- church officials
- malcontents
- clowns
- mad people
- women
- the working classes
- the lover
- supernatural figures.

Rulers
Social inequality

Elizabethan and Jacobean drama depicts a world in which social and political inequality are the norm. There is likely to be at least one ruler of the society in your play.

Obedience

There is no democracy for the characters in your drama. The political expectation, or at least the social norm, of the play is that the ruler must be obeyed. The character of the ruler can be aristocratic (titled) or clerical (a high-ranking church official), or both. Your ruler might be presented as strong and secure or weak and endangered. Strong or weak, they are all presented with flaws.

Tragedy or tragic history

If the ruler is also presented as the tragic hero, their flaws are their downfall and they inevitably die. Remember that it is necessary for their presentation to be a sympathetic one, even if they commit terrible acts. For example, King Lear, Edward II and Richard II.

The ruler might be a minor character who is necessary for the resolution in the outcome of the play and has thematic functions, such as Malcolm in *Macbeth* or Antonio in *The Revenger's Tragedy*.

Comedy

The role of the ruler is to impose their authority and restore order by the end. You might not see or hear much from or even about them until they are needed for the comic resolution of the ending – for example, Theseus in *A Midsummer Night's Dream*. They might also be presented as partly responsible for the initial cause of disorder. Because they are in charge, they have the power to dispense and escape punishment – for example, the Duke in *Measure for Measure*. Their rule or authority might be legal and moral rather than royal, such as 1st Avocatore, the magistrate in *Volpone*, who sentences Volpone and Mosca for their crimes.

Tragi-comedy

The ruler is presented as flawed, like a tragic hero, but the anagnorisis they experience is achieved in time to deliver a comic ending. They learn how to redeem themselves through wisdom or compromise – for example, Prospero in *The Tempest*.

Central or minor characters

Rulers can be central characters, as they often are in tragedy and tragi-comedy, or they can be presented as shadowy, background figures – as they often are in comedy – to provide a guiding framework for matters of social order, duty, personal responsibility and law enforcement when events go awry. Alternatively, the play can determine that your rulers are challenged, deposed, killed or avenged according to the conventions of the genre or the ideas of the dramatist.

Corruption

If the ruler is presented as irredeemably corrupt, he is unlikely to be identified as the hero. For example, Claudius in *Hamlet* or Brachiano in *The White Devil*. The social contexts of Elizabethan and Jacobean drama required honourable behaviour and attitudes from its heroes. The original audience would have been aware of the honour codes in their contemporary society and their views of the hero are likely to have been filtered through these beliefs.

Power

Where power, especially political power, is a main theme in your play, the ruler might be presented in conflict, with another ruler, usurper or avenger who can be presented as justified, or not, in the world of the play. This is true of Marlowe's *Edward II*, Shakespeare's Roman plays and those with titular kings. There might be battles, scheming or overthrows in your plot. The action is likely to centre on the power struggle for rule in the world of the play by its end. If your rulers engage in this power struggle, what happens to them in the play?

King Lear asserts his authority over his daughters and court

Links

For more information, see Chapter 5, 'The importance of tragic inevitability' (page 35) and 'Remember': 'Catharsis' (page 34).

Links

For more information, see Chapter 5, 'Tragedy': 'Responding to the tragic hero' (page 34) and 'Comedy': 'Tragi-comedy' (page 43).

Remember

Rulers

Rulers can be presented in many ways, depending on the needs of the plot and themes of the play. For example, they can be benevolent, foolish, cruel, evil or noble. Which are yours?

Think about it

Rulers and the ending

Consider the ending of your play. Which character is presented as the ruler? How does their speech and action present views of how to behave in the world of the play? Is rule ever shared in your play? How do your findings reflect the Elizabethan and Jacobean social and political contexts?

Link

For more information, see Chapter 7, 'Significant themes in context': 'Behaviour codes': 'Honour' (page 57).

David Tennant as the tragic hero Hamlet, contemplates mortality

Bosola uncovers the Duchess of Malfi's secret pregnancy for villainous ends

Support and opposition

It is likely that your ruling character has supporters and opponents amongst the other characters. These can be important or minor characters in the plot but if they contribute to your understanding of the behaviour and attitudes of the ruler, the other character has a dramatic significance in the presentation of the ruler in your play.

Activity 3

The ruler in your play

Consider the characterisation of the ruler in your play. If there is a change of ruler, do this activity for each of them. Use the bullet points from Activity 1 to help you.

1. How is the dramatist characterising the ruler in the play?

2. How does their characterisation demonstrate the Elizabethan and Jacobean contexts operating on your ruling character?

Heroes and villains

The hero

The hero who is not a ruler has limited power initially and any that is gained is lost by the end. The plot and genre determine how the power-struggle ends for the hero who is not a ruler. For example, Doctor Faustus, Hamlet and Macbeth. The fact that these characters are titular heroes shows you that the focus of the play is on their fortunes and outcomes. They are the most important characters in these plays, not their rulers: the Devil, King Claudius and King Duncan.

The villain

The villain in your play might also be the ruler. In a comedy or a tragedy, the role of the villain is to disturb and destroy the hero – and with it, social harmony or order.

Villains in a tragedy are successful in defeating the hero, up to a point, and they have a serious impact on the tragic outcomes of the play. Villains in a comedy attempt social disruption but do not succeed in their selfish or peevish goals. Villains are made to pay for their crimes – the severity of the punishment depends on the genre, how much suffering they have caused and the impact on those they tormented.

For example, in the tragedy of *Edward II*, Mortimer Junior is presented with some potentially honourable intentions but is ultimately corrupt and commits treason in the world of the play, through his part in the murder of the king. His punishment is execution. In Jonson's satiric comedy, *Volpone* – which means 'the fox' – is the central character. He is a conman and, like a fox, a wily predator. The dramatic significance of his name tells us that he is clever and outwits his victims – for a while. Consequently, at the outcome, his punishment is harsh. He is publicly humiliated, made to help the society he deceived and stripped of the wealth he has stolen. Volpone's servant, Mosca, however, is imprisoned for life. (Different punishment according to social class is a contemporary political context that features in drama from the period.)

Villains are often presented as suffering from envy, jealousy, greed or covetousness – unchristian attitudes in the Christian contexts of

Elizabethan and Jacobean societies. Others are presented with a genuine grievance of unjust treatment: perhaps cruelty, rejection or abandonment. For example, Edmond in *King Lear*. Such presentations provide a motive for villainous actions – even if the character does not receive forgiveness in the world of the play or a change in their fortunes when they are discovered. Can you identify any villains in your plays?

Hero or villain?

Later Jacobean plays – especially the tragedies of Middleton, *The Revenger's Tragedy*, of Webster, *The White Devil*, and of Ford, *'Tis Pity She's a Whore* – often blur the boundaries of hero and villain. Without a clear tragic hero, these tragedies present a world in which moral lines appear blurred, social order is in disarray, honour codes have been forgotten and there are few characters to admire. A Shakespearian example is Angelo in *Measure for Measure*.

Church officials and religious figures

Your play might include characters that represent the Church such as priests, friars, bishops, cardinals or even the Pope. If they are very high-ranking, they might also be the ruler in your play, such as the Cardinal in *The Duchess of Malfi*. Your play can present them as righteous, sycophantic or corrupt, invested with either moral authority or dereliction of duty in the actions and ideas of the plays.

If the presentation is righteous, the religious character attempts to influence the behaviour of characters in moral danger to save their souls and change their course of action. If the presentation is corrupt, the religious character is involved in acts viewed as sinful by the society in the play and the Elizabethan or Jacobean audience watching them. Friars are presented more ambiguously. For example, the goodly but ineffective Friar Bonaventura in *'Tis Pity She's a Whore*, the Friars in *Doctor Faustus* and the compliant Friar Thomas in *Measure for Measure*.

Malcontents

A malcontent is usually characterised by his ill-will towards the other characters. Malcontents are presented as restless and unhappy with their (often social) status in the world of the play. These characters are constructed to seek change in their world by underhand means and can be presented as spies, panders, melancholics and meddlers. For example, Vindice in *The Revenger's Tragedy*. They are often presented unsympathetically when they are also villains, however minor. Some malcontents might come to repent or feel pity or sympathy for the characters they torment. For example, Bosola and Flamineo in Webster's *The Duchess of Malfi* and *The White Devil*.

Sympathy for the malcontent

Malcontents attract more audience sympathy when they represent or comment on the wider social and political injustices that the dramatist explores in the play. It is hard for an audience to judge a malcontent against a backdrop of prejudice and corruption from which they suffer. This is noticeable in the tragedies of Middleton and Webster. In a comedy, the tone is lighter and they might simply be mocked.

The outsider

Malcontents are all outsiders, sometimes lonely or friendless, in the society they seek to join or change. For example, Jaques in *As You Like It*. Their role

Link

For more information, see Chapter 7, 'Behaviour codes': 'The law and punishment' (page 56).

Think about it

Plays that lack an identifiable hero

Why might the later Jacobean tragedies struggle to present an identifiable tragic hero? Does the lack of an identifiable hero reveal any of the social and political contexts of the time?

Presenting religious figures

How does your play present religious figures? If they are absent from the play, what might that suggest?

Faustus and Mephistopheles bait the Pope with magic in *Doctor Faustus*

Key terms

Pander: a Jacobean pimp.

Melancholic: a thoughtful, introverted loner.

Remember

The Catholic Church

The reputation of the Catholic Church was in crisis in England during the Elizabethan and Jacobean periods. Presentations of Catholic clergy reflect this in your plays. The presentation of lascivious and sexually corrupted top churchmen (usually Italian) is a popular characterisation.

Did you know?

Surprising malcontents
The tragic hero Hamlet is characterised as an unhappy melancholic seeking change subversively. Some critics have argued that he is presented as the malcontent in the play.

Link

For more information, see Chapter 5, 'Comedy': 'Stock characters' (page 42).

Link

For more information, see Chapter 9, 'Dramatic techniques' (page 81).

Castrone, Androgyno and Nano from *Volpone*

Link

For more information, see Chapter 12, 'Key influences on comedy': '*Commedia dell'Arte*' (page 106).

is often characterised by secret missions or isolated errands. They observe other characters, often speaking in asides and building a relationship with the audience, as if they know they are in a play, such as Bosola in *The Duchess of Malfi*. Their point of view is clear to the audience – whether or not it is admired – but not to the other characters.

Clowns

Shakespeare

Clowns or jesters have an important role in Shakespeare's Elizabethan and Jacobean plays. They appear in his comedy, tragedy and tragi-comedy. Shakespeare uses this character type in a variety of ways. His clowns and jesters might engage in farcical and slapstick actions that amuse or inconvenience the other characters in the play such as Trinculo in his Jacobean tragi-comedy, *The Tempest*. In other plays, his clowns are vital to the plot and its outcome. For example, Puck in *A Midsummer Night's Dream*. Clowns are often important in the creation of chaos and disorder in Elizabethan comedy but are not seen as malicious or ill-meaning.

The social status of the clown

In some plays, the jester, or fool, is a 'live-in' personal entertainer for the head of an aristocratic household, such as Touchstone in *As You Like It*. Far from being a foolish character, jesters are presented as perceptive and witty. The jester might develop a personal bond with their employer who comes to rely on their shrewd, frank interpretation of the chaotic world presented in the play. Their unusual closeness to the aristocracy – they otherwise have a low social status – protects them from the usual hardships of their class. Shakespeare's construct of Fool in the tragedy of *King Lear* is a sophisticated treatment of intimacy and humanity in the relationship between rulers and servants. As a result, Fool has a relative position of privilege. As you can see, this character type functions in opposite ways to the malcontent.

Marlowe

In Marlowe's Elizabethan tragedy of *Doctor Faustus*, Robin the clown is constructed to provide comic relief from the tragic main plot and to mimic and comment on the serious themes explored in the tragic plot.

The clown as social commentator

Clowns are presented with the jovial cover of a joker or the pitiful disguise of an imbecile. If the clown is presented as stupid, the characters – and the audience – can dismiss their words as unimportant ramblings. If the clown is presented as funny, the characters – and the audience – can laugh at them and their provocative remarks. Consequently, they are presented as unthreatening to the powerful characters – and to the audience.

This is an ironic presentation, as the clown is often used as a social commentator. He shares with other characters and the audience, his views on what happens in the play – without suffering punishment or execution for being out-spoken. For example, Fool in *King Lear* is presented as the truth-teller, and Feste's songs provide a candid commentary on events in *Twelfth Night*.

Jonson

Jonson uses clowns in his Jacobean comedy *Volpone* as figures of fun. His characters Nano, Castrone and Androgyno are dressed in masks and plumes and described as a Dwarf, a Eunuch and a Hermaphrodite.

The end of the clown

In Jacobean revenge tragedy, the character type of a clown has disappeared. It is replaced by comic behaviour and language from the tragic characters. These episodes of comic relief are presented as graphic horror scenes as the dramatists question the conventions of the revenge subgenre and respond to their own social and political contexts.

Mad people

Men and women who go mad are an important character type in Elizabethan and Jacobean tragedy. Madness is presented as the moral decline of a character who goes mad or/and of their contemporary society. Madness ends with death, often suicide. Mad characters are not presented as people to receive treatment or rehabilitation. They are constructed to die to symbolise for the audience the extent and effects of moral and social chaos in the play. For example, in Shakespeare's tragedies Lady Macbeth is presented as a cause of the chaos while Ophelia is presented as a victim of the chaos.

Can you identify madness in any characters from your play?

The women

Character types

The category of 'The women' as a character type is contentious in itself. There is no character type of 'The men'. In the 18 Elizabethan and Jacobean plays discussed in this book, the dramatists construct male characters that are rulers, heroes, villains, church officials, malcontents, fools and clowns, madmen or supernatural figures. The only character types that women share with men in these plays are all Shakespearian: the villains – for example, Regan and Goneril in *King Lear;* the mad people – for example, the crushed innocence of Shakespeare's Ophelia in *Hamlet;* the supernatural figures – for example, the Witches in *Macbeth;* lowly religious officials – for example, the novice Isabella in *Measure for Measure.*

Women, like men, are presented as lovers or working class across the plays but they are never presented as rulers, clowns or malcontents in drama from this period. They are rarely the heroes. A woman can have a significant role and be presented as an interesting character with heroic potential but she is not in charge of the political and social world in the play. For example, Vittoria in *The White Devil.*

Women are presented as mothers, daughters and wives but these roles are in relation to the fathers, sons and husbands in their family. The women are not in charge of this institution either. For example, Vindice's mother Gratiana in *The Revenger's Tragedy* and Hamlet's mother Gertrude.

The title of the play

Titular characters of Elizabethan and Jacobean plays are usually male, for example *Hamlet.* The drama of this period focuses primarily on the fortunes and influence of a man.

Of all the plays we consider, there is one titular heroine where the primary focus is on the fortunes of a female character: Webster's *The Duchess of Malfi.* However, as a woman in a patriarchal system, she is not the ruler. Even as a duchess, she cannot rule or make independent choices, including

Think about it

Presentations of the clown

How might Shakespeare or Marlowe use the characterisation of a clown to comment on shocking or controversial events in Elizabethan or Jacobean society?

Why do you think that the role of the clown is absent from Jacobean revenge tragedies by Middleton, Webster and Ford? Which of their characters typify any of the ways in which clowns can be characterised?

Did you know?

'Hieronimo is mad againe'
This is the sub-title of Kyd's play, *The Spanish Tragedy.* Hieronimo is the revenge hero, driven to suicidal distraction by grief at the unpunished murder of his son.

Links

For more information, see Chapter 7, 'Significant themes in context': 'Chaos and madness' (page 59) and Chapter 12, 'Key influences on tragedy' (page 104).

whom she can marry. This social context is the framework for her tragedy. The only other play we consider from this period that references a female character in the title is the latest Jacobean play, Ford's *'Tis Pity She's a Whore*. The title is not encouraging as a presentation of a heroine, especially when you consider her fate.

Gender inequality in context

Gender inequality must be viewed in Elizabethan and Jacobean contexts. Women had no political power or financial independence at the time. Social freedom was limited and sexual encounters were forbidden and came at a price, especially if discovered. Women were legally the property of the man sworn to protect them, from the father to the husband. This left only one respectable social role for women to occupy: wife, to whichever man was the woman's social match. If they were not yet married, the procurement of a suitable suitor was a woman's main activity. In times of war, strife and violent conflict, women had even less to do but more to fear as they had limited power or command. The presentations of aristocratic women in your plays are likely to represent these contexts. The non-aristocratic women followed the same path but lower down the social hierarchy from the merchant class to the working class. Their individual lives were not the principal stuff of plays that you are studying from this period.

Personality, intelligence, personal power

Women then, as now, had three things going for them: personality, intelligence and personal power. Personality, as much as circumstance, determines your response to the social structures. As a result, the women in your plays can be characterised as strong or weak, empowered or victimised. Intelligent ideas and behaviour help to secure greater social freedom and opportunities. Personal power is found in personal relationships. A woman who has the ear or the love of (in their case) a man, can influence how the hierarchy operates in the house.

The playwrights could model their women on the social roles permitted at the time or they could construct a female character with personality, intelligence and personal power, whatever her social and political standing. Shakespeare creates women with these survival skills: in the comedies, Viola and Rosalind in *Twelfth Night* and *As You Like It*, and in the tragedies, Cordelia in *King Lear* and Lady Macbeth. Webster creates the defiant Duchess and the articulate Vittoria in *The White Devil*. Middleton constructs the feisty and resistant Castiza, sister to Vindice, in *The Revenger's Tragedy*. These are all presented as assertive women, albeit within the social and political gender constraints of the world inside and outside of the play.

Female stereotypes

You can detect patterns of the social and political presentations of women in drama from this period – but do not stereotype or generalise the presentation of the women in your play. Despite social and political obstacles, they are presented with more options than you might think. The female characters might not escape the macro contexts of the period that are revealed in the world of the plays but they can be characterised through their attempts to challenge, outwit or overcome the status quo.

Did you know?

The queen and inequality for women

The fact that Elizabeth I was a woman had no impact on the inequality of women of any social class during her reign. The social, political and legal systems were still patriarchal in England. This applied even to the queen – she was only the ruler because her father, Henry VIII, had no surviving male heir to the throne. He had the power, as a king in a patriarchy, to kill each of his wives who did not provide him with a male heir.

Vittoria from *The White Devil*

Activity 4

The women in your play
Consider the women characters in your play. Use the bullet points from Activity 1 for each female character.

1. How does the dramatist characterise each of the women?

2. How do their characterisations demonstrate the Elizabethan and Jacobean contexts operating on the female characters in your play/s?

The working classes

Stereotypes
The working classes have a low social status and no political power in the drama of the period. You can observe presentations of stereotypical working-class characters who embody urban sleaze, for example Mosca the Parasite in *Volpone*, or as rural idiots, for example the workers/players in *A Midsummer Night's Dream*.

Thematic function
Elizabethan and Jacobean dramatic plots do not focus primarily on presentations of working-class hardship or grief. Characterisations of the working class, from the plays we explore, might have a thematic function and contribute to the development of characters with a higher social and political status in the play. Shakespeare and Marlowe's clowns and fools have this dramatic function. For example, Robin in *Doctor Faustus* and the gravediggers in *Hamlet*.

Minor characters
The working class are often minor characters and sometimes presented in groups, rather than as significant individuals. Shakespeare presents them in a work role: the shepherds/esses in *As You Like It*, the sailors in *Twelfth Night* and the drunken butler, Stephano, in *The Tempest*.

More often, the working class occupies one role in drama from this period: servant, by which their character is named. For example, in *Richard II*, *The White Devil* and *The Duchess of Malfi*.

The dramatic function of servants
In the Jacobean revenge tragedies there are named servants. They are constructed to contribute to the fortunes of the characters they serve. In *The Spanish Tragedy* and *The White Devil*, the servants betray those whom they serve to their enemies. In *'Tis Pity She's a Whore*, Vasques is loyal to Lord Soranzo but his violent actions, motivated in part by servitude, contribute to the fall of Annabella.

Power and the working class
The working class is presented as having some power en masse – for example, as a fear-arousing mob in *Hamlet* – and as socially influential prostitutes and madams – such as Mistress Overdone in *Measure for Measure*. However, working-class voices do not drive the main plot or themes in the drama of this period.

Webster's plays and social class
Marlowe presents a hero with 'parents base of stock' in *Doctor Faustus* (Prologue, line 12) and Jonson's city comedies develop presentations of

Links

For more information, see Chapter 2, 'The macro contexts': 'Political backgrounds' (page 10), Chapter 4, 'Remember': 'The Divine Rights of Kings' (page 24), 'Did you know?': 'The Great Chain of Being' (page 25) and Chapter 7, 'Significant themes in context': 'Power' (page 58).

Did you know?

City comedy
There are excellent examples of drama from this period, set in a contemporary Jacobean London, that do focus on the individual fortunes of working-class central characters.

Further reading

City comedies
Ben Jonson, *The Alchemist* (c.1610)

Thomas Middleton, *A Chaste Maid in Cheapside* (c.1611–1613)

Think about it

The working class in drama and context
Identify the presentations of the working-class characters in your play. How do their fortunes change in the development of the plot? How are they thematically significant? How are they important to the outcome of the play? How do their presentations reveal the social and political contexts of the time?

Link

For more information on stock characters, see Chapter 5, 'Literary contexts' (pages 33–44).

Link

For more information, see Chapter 4, 'The Renaissance context': 'Shifting religious attitudes and beliefs' (page 25).

working-class individuals. However, the presentation of social class in tragedy changes with Middleton and Webster. In *The Revenger's Tragedy*, *The Duchess of Malfi* and *The White Devil*, against the backdrop of the rise of the merchant class, we see the struggles and profiles of the middle class represented alongside the aristocracy.

Webster uses the characters of stewards and secretaries to the aristocracy to present the unhappy fate of the middle class in his plays. The aspirational Antonio becomes the socially unacceptable husband of the Duchess of Malfi. Flamineo, a fallen gentleman, commits such treachery, with the Duke Brachiano, that his own sister and lover attempt his murder. Webster explores their individual lives rather than grouping them together as one mass social class. As a result, he creates complex and sympathetic middle-class characters that are untypical of tragedy in the Elizabethan and Jacobean period.

How do you think Webster's choices reflect the shifting social-class structures in Elizabethan and Jacobean society?

The lover
In your plays, any of the character types described above could be presented as a lover. The genre of comedy or tragedy determines how that love develops and ends. The presentation of social and political constraints of class and marriage determines how the lover is presented in the play and their relative importance to the plot.

Supernatural figures
Supernatural figures abound in your plays. Elizabethan and Jacobean beliefs in the after-life and attitudes to the spirit world determined the presentation of supernatural characters in this period.

Consider in your play the presence of:

- ghosts – feature in many Elizabethan and Jacobean revenge tragedies of the period. They are never good news

- morality figures – in Elizabethan tragedy, for example Good and Bad Angels

- the personification of human qualities – in Elizabethan tragedy. For example, Revenge or The Seven Deadly Sins

- devils or angels, present or summoned

- fairies – Elizabethan pastoral comedy often features creatures from the woodland spirit world

- witches, sorcerers and magicians – alive, but endowed with supernatural powers such as prophesy.

Consider these questions:

- How important are supernatural characters in the plot and themes of your play?

- How does their presence signify the social, cultural and political contexts at work on the drama of the period?

- How are these supernatural characterisations different across the genres and between the Elizabethan and the Jacobean periods?

The three witches from *Macbeth*

The relationship between context and character in your text

Applying context questions 1

Characterisation

Read the three following extracts. Use the bullet points from Activities 1 and 2, and the section 'Significant character types in context', to help you.

1. Analyse how each character is presented in each extract.

2. Compare and contrast each characterisation and character type, within and across each extract.

3. Consider your own plays. Select an extract of 20–50 lines that explores one of the character types that you identify in the extracts. Analyse how your extract explores characterisation and character type in the macro and literary contexts of your play. Do this for each character in your chosen extracts.

4. Compare and contrast how you respond to the presentations of each character across the extracts below and from your own plays. Analyse how the context of reception influences your responses.

Extract 1

William Shakespeare, *King Lear*

This extract is from the beginning of the play. King Lear is old and without a son and heir so decides to divide his kingdom between his three daughters. In exchange for his gift, they must tell him how much they love him as proof of their loyalty. Cordelia, the youngest and unmarried, is devoted to her father. Her two elder married sisters are dishonest and selfish. They have finished declaring their love to their father and now it is Cordelia's turn. The outcome of this dialogue sets the tragic plot of conflict in motion.

LEAR
What can you say to draw
A third more opulent than your sisters? Speak.

CORDELIA
Nothing, my lord.

LEAR
Nothing?

CORDELIA
Nothing.

LEAR
Nothing will come of nothing, speak again.

CORDELIA
Unhappy that I am, I cannot heave
My heart into my mouth: I love your majesty
According to my bond, no more nor less.

LEAR
How, how, Cordelia? Mend your speech a little,
Lest you may mar your fortunes.

CORDELIA   Good my lord,
You have begot me, bred me, loved me. I
Return those duties back as are right fit,
Obey you, love you, and most honour you.
Why have my sisters husbands, if they say
They love you all? Happily, when I shall wed,
That lord whose hand must take my plight shall carry
Half my love with him, half my care and duty.
Sure, I shall never marry like my sisters.

LEAR
But goes thy heart with this?

CORDELIA   Ay, my good lord.

LEAR
So young, and so untender?

CORDELIA
So young, my lord, and true.

LEAR
Let it be so, thy truth then be thy dower.

King Lear by William Shakespeare (1608). Act 1, Scene 1, lines 80–102

Extract 2

Christopher Marlowe, *Doctor Faustus*

This extract is from the ending of the play. Faustus, alone, awaits his fate: descent into hell with Lucifer the Devil, his payment for 24 years of magic powers on Earth, after using magic books to summon him.

FAUSTUS
Let Faustus live in hell a thousand years,
A hundred thousand, and at last be saved.
No end is limited to damned souls.
Why wert thou not a creature wanting soul?
Or why is this immortal that thou hast?
O, Pythagoras' *metempsychosis*, were that true,
This soul should fly from me and I be changed
Into some brutish beast.
All beasts are happy, for, when they die,
Their souls are soon dissolved in elements;
But mine must live still to be plagued in hell.
Curst be the parents that engendered me!
No, Faustus, curse thyself. Curse Lucifer,
That hath deprived thee of the joys of heaven.
                    The clock strikes twelve
It strikes, it strikes! Now, body, turn to air,
Or Lucifer will bear thee quick to hell.
O soul, be changed into small waterdrops,
And fall into the ocean, ne'er be found!
Thunder, and enter the Devils
O, mercy, heaven, look not so fierce on me!
Adders and serpents, let me breathe a while!
Ugly hell, gape not. Come not, Lucifer!
I'll burn my books. O, Mephistopheles!
                    Exeunt

Doctor Faustus by Christopher Marlowe, 'B text'. Act 5, Scene 2, lines 163–185

Extract 3
John Webster, *The White Devil*

This extract is from the latter part of the play. Duke Brachiano has killed his innocent wife to begin a sexual liaison, then marriage, to Vittoria, whose husband he also killed. Flamineo is Brachiano's secretary and Vittoria's brother, whom he procured for the Duke. Flamineo is a complex character and this episode reveals only some aspects of his characterisations. At this point in the play, Brachiano falsely suspects that Vittoria is unfaithful to him and summons Flamineo to bring her to him.

BRACHIANO
In you pander!

FLAMINEO
[*Facing him*] What me, my lord, am I your dog?

BRACHIANO
A bloodhound: do you brave? Do you stand me?

FLAMINEO
Stand you? Let those that have diseases run;
I need no plasters.

BRACHIANO
Would you be kicked?

FLAMINEO   Would you have your neck broke?
I tell you duke, I am not in Russia;
My shins must be kept whole.

BRACHIANO   Do you know me?

FLAMINEO
O my lord! Methodically.
As in this world there are degrees of evils:
So in this world there are degrees of devils.
You're a great Duke; I your poor secretary.
I do now look for a Spanish fig, or an Italian sallet daily.

BRACHIANO
Pander, ply your convoy, and leave your prating.

FLAMINEO
All your kindness to me is like that miserable courtesy of Polyphemus to Ulysses; you reserve me to be devoured last. You would dig turves out of my grave to feed your larks: that would be music to you. Come, I'll lead you to her.   [*Walks backwards*]

BRACHIANO
Do you face me?

FLAMINEO
O sir, I would not go before a politic enemy with my Back towards him, though there were behind me a whirlpool.

Enter VITTORIA to BRACHIANO and FLAMINEO

The White Devil by John Webster (1609–1612). Act 4, Scene 2, lines 47–69

Summary

In this chapter, you have considered:

- a definition of characterisation
- ways in which to analyse character
- significant character types in context
- how to analyse the relationship between context and character in the texts and contexts.

9 Actors and acting

Chapter aims

In this chapter we focus on the contextual significance of actors and acting in Elizabethan and Jacobean drama. We will explore:

- the reputation of actors
- the use of boy players
- acting styles
- dramatic techniques
- how to contextualise 'actors and acting' in your play.

Link

For more information, see Chapter 11, 'Theatres' (pages 96–103).

Did you know?

Actors and the plague
In 1572, the city authorities, the Mayor and Corporation of London, banned plays for health and safety reasons. In 1575 they expelled all actors from the city of London. the new theatres, including the Globe, were built just outside of the city limits.

Think about it

Players, unrest and the plague
Can you compare this Elizabethan social attitude and religious belief – blaming a group of people for social unrest or fatal diseases – with any of our contemporary attitudes to a social, racial or other group?

Link

For more information, see Chapter 11, 'The patronage of theatre companies' (page 101).

The reputation of actors

In the early Elizabethan era, actors had a bad reputation and were seen as untrustworthy scoundrels, not to be taken seriously. This attitude was mostly propagated by the Church and it persisted throughout the Elizabethan era. The reputation of actors improved with the opening of specially built playhouses: firstly, the Theatre in 1576 and, famously, the Globe in 1599. The popularity of the theatre came to have more influence than the bad reputation of actors but players and playhouses were still blamed for all manner of social evils.

A danger to society

Playhouses were said to create rowdy disturbances in a crowd, increase late-night 'traffic' and encourage licentious behaviour of wanton sexuality and drunkenness. It was believed that playhouses spread, and even caused, the plague as a punishment from God for sin.

As Puritanism grew, actors and acting were considered too risqué to be tolerated by the conservative elements of Elizabethan society.

Prejudice towards Jacobean actors eased as theatre became the social and leisure activity of choice but it was still not seen as a decent trade. However, the reputation of actors began to change as the populace of London was offered an intensive volume of high-quality theatre.

Actors and celebrity status

Acting had initially been a poorly paid job, especially for the apprenticed boy players. But as an actor was paid according to standing in the theatre company, based on his popularity and frequency of appearance, the celebrated actors became the stars of their day. The actors Richard Burbage and Edward Alleyn, who were also theatre managers, were 'A-listers' with the salary to match. William Shakespeare had shares in the Globe and became wealthy on the profits.

Royal protection and the theatre

The theatre had powerful friends – as you know, James I and Elizabeth I loved the theatre. Throughout the Elizabethan and Jacobean eras, theatre companies were protected by the monarch and by members of the aristocracy and government.

How that protection operated under Elizabeth I was different from how it functioned under James I but the outcome was the same. Neither the Church, the London City Corporation nor the opinion of the Puritans could stand in the way of a monarch and a favourite pastime: play-watching. For the actors of the day, there was a tension between the royal approach – approval, protection and support – and the religious and political forces amassed against them – disapproval, condemnation and the desire to dismantle the profession and its venues. Eventually, the monarchy lost this power struggle and with it the actors. The theatres were closed down in 1642 when the Puritans took power from Charles I in the Civil Wars.

Richard Burbage and Edward Alleyn

Links

For more information, see Chapter 4, 'Ruling English monarchs 1590–1640': 'Monarchy in crisis' and 'Theatre in crisis' (page 24) and Chapter 13, 'Chronology of events' (page 107).

Boy players

Women were forbidden from acting in this period of English drama. It was not until the 1660s, with the restoration of the monarchy and Charles II, that women acting in plays became acceptable.

However, someone had to play the female parts, especially in the romantic and pastoral comedies with plots of love and marriage. Boy players took these roles within apprenticeships to the adult male players whom they would one day join and replace. Boy players lived with their master, did his bidding and gave him their wages for food, accommodation and tutoring in their parts. There were no degrees in stagecraft and drama at university or independent jobs as a theatre professional. They did get to dress up but always for the same part: the wife, lover, daughter or sister of a male character.

Effects on the text

The dramatists developed a variety of strategies to manage the 'boy player' factor in performance. Limited appearances of female characters were common in the plays. Roles for boys were developed that required more emotional, than physical, acting in the tragedies. Cross-dressing in the comedies helped to suspend disbelief of boys playing women in the love scenes.

Acting styles

Now you have some knowledge of the off-stage fortunes, the social and political contexts, of the male players in the Elizabethan and Jacobean period. Let us consider a literary context – acting styles.

Overacting

Overacting was a mainstay style in the Elizabethan period. Poor acoustics in the outside theatre and a large, noisy crowd of **groundlings** meant that quiet, tender or subtle speeches and dialogue could be lost on many audience members. The pitfalls of this acting style might have denied the audience some of the exquisitely crafted verse and intricate language. Shakespeare raises the limitations of overacting in *Hamlet*.

Think about it

Women actors in context

In 1629 (around the time that John Ford was beginning to write his play *'Tis Pity She's a Whore*), women actors attempted to perform at the Blackfriars Theatre in London. They belonged to a visiting French mixed-sex theatre company. The women were booed and bombarded off the stage. Why do you think that might have been?

Key term

Groundling someone too poor to buy a seat, who stood in the cramped open-air pit to watch the play.

Link

For more information, see Chapter 11, 'The significance of indoor and outdoor spaces' (page 100).

Did you know?

Acting schedules
The competition was so tough in this Golden Age of the theatre that to attract audiences, a theatre had to change plays constantly. The Globe records show that between 10 and 12 plays a fortnight were often performed, giving little time for rehearsal or for learning lines. Cue acting and cue scripting were common.

Key terms

Cue acting a backstage prompt whispered the actor's lines before he had to perform them.

Cue scripting the actor only saw the lines for his own part.

Extract 1
William Shakespeare, *Hamlet*

This extract is from the middle of the play where Hamlet speaks to an acting troupe performing at the palace. In an earlier episode, he sees their acting styles and is angry with himself as they act out emotions so convincingly when he cannot be swept to revenge by his genuine feelings. He cites the players as the motivation to spur him on. In this extract, he is instructing the First Player in the acting styles he wants them to use when they perform for the king.

Enter Hamlet and the Players

HAMLET
Speak the speech, I pray you, as I pronounced
it to you, trippingly on the tongue. But if you mouth it
as many of our players do, I had as lief the town crier
spoke my lines. Nor do not saw the air too much with
your hand, thus. But use all gently. For in the very tor-
rent, tempest, and as I may say, whirlwind of your
passion, you must acquire and beget a temperance that
may give it smoothness. O, it offends me to the soul to
hear a robustious periwig-pated fellow to tear a passion to
tatters, to very rags, to split the ears of the groundlings,
who for the most part are capable of nothing but in-
explicable dumb shows and noise. I would have such a
fellow whipped for o'erdoing Termagant. It out-Herods
Herod. Pray you avoid it.

FIRST PLAYER
I warrant your honour.

HAMLET
Be not too tame neither. But let your own dis-
cretion be your tutor. Suit the action to the word, the
word to the action, with this special observance, that
you o'erstep not the modesty of nature. For anything so
o'erdone is from the purpose of playing, whose end,
both at the first and now, was and is to hold, as 'twere,
the mirror up to nature, to show virtue her own feature,
scorn her own image, and the very age and body of the
time his form and pressure.

Hamlet by William Shakespeare (1603). Act 3, Scene 2, lines 1–24

Applying context questions 1

Acting styles
Read the extract from *Hamlet* and answer the following questions:

- How does the presentation of acting reflect the popular acting styles used at the time?

- How do you think Shakespeare is responding to the acting style of 'overacting'?

- How does your own play/s present the role and significance of acting styles?

- How does your dramatist/s respond to the acting style of 'overacting'?

Dramatic techniques

Some dramatic techniques developed by the dramatists of this period are:

- the play within the play
- the use of acting, spying and disguise
- the soliloquy and the aside.

None of these features is new to the Elizabethan and Jacobean period but they are important literary contexts in your drama.

A modern audience responds to a performance at the Globe

The play within the play

The dramatic technique of 'a play within the play' is used in the construction of plot and structure in Elizabethan and Jacobean plays from this period. The audience learns more about the themes and characters by observing this technique as it reflects the main concerns in the play.

A subplot achieves a similar effect but the 'play' technique offers more with its two audiences: you and the other characters. Watching characters respond to the 'play' shows the audience more about their characterisation.

The play within the play is used in Shakespearian Elizabethan comedy as a moral instruction as well as to entertain the characters in the world of the play, such as in *A Midsummer Night's Dream*. In tragedy, it is important for setting or changing the mood of your play and can direct the audience to the ways in which themes will develop. For example, in Shakespeare's *Hamlet* and in Kyd's *The Spanish Tragedy*.

Dumb show

A dumb show is highly ritualised and self-consciously staged, involving a procession of central characters across the stage, often with torches and sometimes in masks. It might be used as a way to introduce supernatural elements into your play, to present several plot developments using limited stage time or to develop an important theme. A dumb show can be used

Did you know?

Meta-theatre
This is the term we give to the dramatic technique of a play within the play. It applies to any dramatic construct where the characters are aware that they participate in a performance, both as audiences and actors.

The 'play within the play' from *Hamlet*

to show murders to the audience, either as part of the main plot or as a mirror and comment on the murders in the main plot. The dumb show is a mainstay of revenge tragedy and is used by Kyd, Webster, Middleton and Ford.

Acting out a role: spying, lying and dissembling
The context of deception

The context of your plays is a society in which people deceive one another in law, court, marriage, business and politics. Within the play, plotting, deception, disguise and playing roles are dramatic devices used to develop and complicate the plot for tragic or comic purposes, as well as having thematic importance. Spying has dramatic significance as it shapes the plot and structure of the play. Deception is essential to the subgenres of revenge tragedy and romantic comedy.

Deception in the plays

Pretending to be someone or something you are not, through a physical disguise or concealing your identity or feelings, is a key feature of Elizabethan and Jacobean drama. It can reveal the extent of sorrow, danger, moral breakdown or social collapse presented in the world of the play – and maybe in the social and political world outside of the play. Many of your characters are presented in a deceptive role and act out behaviour and speech for other characters in order to uncover or hide the truth and the desire for justice.

Deception can be used to meddle or to create chaos, especially in comedy. It might be used to mix comic and tragic messages in tragi-comedy. It might involve the use of macabre or sexual props, especially in tragedy. For example, severed heads, skulls, corpses and skeletons, the cover of darkness or curtains, the donning of a physical disguise or a veil such as the veil that hides Gloriana's skull from the Duke in *The Revenger's Tragedy.*

Spies and lies

Why this gruesome, eerie trickery? The use of pretence is to protect or strip away the layers in your play. Secrecy and deception are embedded in your play, not least the human tendency for self-deception. The technique of acting and pretending – for mischief, deceit and double-cross – is a thrilling aspect of the drama in this period and contributes much to the excitement and tension within the mood of the play.

Dramatic irony

The techniques of acting and pretending rely on another technique: dramatic irony. You belong to the external audience or readership of the text so you are aware of the cloak-and-dagger action. You will be aware of the pretence practised by each of the characters. Characters do not lie to the audience, only to each other – and themselves. Part of the pleasure as you experience these plays is in watching the discovery of secrets and the unravelling of pretences – which you know about all along – and what consequences that has for the world in the play. Let us consider the dramatic techniques used to show you which characters are pretenders.

Link

For more information, see Chapter 4, 'Ruling English monarchs 1590–1640' (page 21).

Think about it

Secrets and pretence
How does the use of dangerous deceit in your play reflect the political or social contexts of the time?

Pretending madness
Do any of the characters in your play pretend to be mad? Why?

Key term

Dramatic irony the audience or reader knows something about a character that the other characters do not know which has significance in the plot.

Soliloquies and asides

A soliloquy or an aside is the way a character speaks privately with the audience, in advance (or instead) of telling the other characters what he or she feels, thinks and plans to do about it.

Soliloquy

A soliloquy is different from a monologue. A character speaks a monologue when other characters are present on stage and might be invited or instructed to listen. A soliloquy is given by a character that is alone on the stage with the complete attention of the audience. It might take the form of a plea, a justification, an explanation, questioning or self-questioning. It could involve plans and schemes for action, a report of action secretly taken or the opinions and descriptions of a character that the speaker is presented to fear, favour, hate or love.

The soliloquy is likely to involve strong emotion or personal searching. Otherwise, it could be spoken in the presence of other characters or would not need your uninterrupted attention. The attention works both ways. As you focus on the character, you receive their complete attention. He or she speaks a soliloquy to the audience and no one else.

Activity 1

The dramatic significance of soliloquy
Consider your own plays. Identify the soliloquies and monologues.

1. Compare how these techniques contribute towards characterisation and development of the plot and themes in your play.

2. How do you respond to the speaker/s of the soliloquy? How do the soliloquies affect **your** relationship with the speaker?

3. How are the macro contexts of your play demonstrated through the use of the soliloquy?

Asides

Asides are remarks made directly to the audience when other characters are on stage. Asides are specifically theatrical in performance because a character must whisper, gesticulate or turn away from the other characters and towards you. They might be subtle or emphatic, even exaggerated, to speak with you but not their fellow characters. Asides are designed as a brief instruction or direction for you to observe a specific aspect of the action, behaviour or speech of other characters as they enact it. An aside is different from dialogue because it is not part of a conversation with other characters. An aside is an opportunity for a character to tell the audience their private point of view even when they are not alone.

Key terms

Soliloquy a character speaks privately to the audience when alone on the stage.

Aside a character speaks privately to the audience whilst other characters are on the stage.

Monologue a character makes a speech to other, listening characters.

Dialogue characters speak with each other.

Think about it

Soliloquy, the speaker and the audience
How is this mutual attention significant for the context of reception in your play? How does the use of soliloquy support what you know about the genre of your play, especially if it is a tragedy?

How to contextualise 'actors and acting' in your play

Applying context questions 2

Dramatic technique and acting styles
Read the two extracts below and answer the following questions.

1. For each extract, analyse how dramatic technique is used to develop plot, theme and character.

2. Compare and contrast the use of dramatic techniques across the extracts.

3. Consider your own plays. Select an extract of 20–50 lines which explores some of the techniques and acting styles, including the significance of boy players, discussed in this chapter. Analyse how your extract uses dramatic technique and acting styles in the literary and macro contexts of your play.

4. Consider your responses to character and plot through the use of speech and soliloquy in all three extracts. Analyse how the context of reception influences your response to each extract.

Extract 1

Thomas Middleton, *The Revenger's Tragedy*

This extract is taken from the penultimate act. The ageing, married Duke, the ruler of an unnamed Italian court, has come to a secret and dark meeting place for sex with a young virgin stranger. The nameless virgin has been procured by the pander Piato who is Vindice in disguise. Vindice has returned from sorrowful travels to seek revenge for the poisoning of his wife, Gloriana, many years before – when she refused the Duke's desire for sex. When the Duke kisses the 'virgin' he finds the veiled skull of Gloriana dressed as an effigy in religious clothing with poison on her 'lips'. Vindice's brother assists him with the distracting perfume and smoke of religious incense to lure the Duke to his fate.

DUKE
Piato! Well done. Hast brought her? What lady is't?

VINDICE
Faith my lord a country lady, a little bashful at first as most of them are, but after the first kiss my lord the worst is past with them: your Grace knows now what you have to do. She's some-what a grave look with her, but –

DUKE
I love that best, conduct her.

VINDICE
[*Aside*] Have at all.

DUKE
In gravest looks the greatest faults seem less:
Give me that sin that's robed in holiness.

VINDICE
[*Aside*] Back with the torch; brother raise the perfumes.

DUKE
How sweet can a duke breathe? Age has no fault.
Pleasure should meet in a perfumed mist.
Lady, sweetly encountered: I came from Court,
I must be bold with you – oh! What's this? Oh!

[*He kisses the skull*]

VINDICE
Royal villain, white devil!

DUKE   Oh!

VINDICE   Brother,

Place the torch here that his affrighted eye-balls
May stare into those hollows. Duke, dost know

Yon dreadful vizard? View it well; 'tis the skull
Of Gloriana, whom thou poisonedst last.

DUKE
Oh 't 'as poisoned me!

VINDICE
Didst not know that till now?

DUKE   What are you two?

The Revenger's Tragedy by Thomas Middleton (1606).
Act 3, Scene 5, lines 131–151

Extract 2

William Shakespeare, *Measure for Measure*

Earlier in the play, the Duke, lax ruler of the city of Vienna, has engineered a way to test Angelo, his deputy, whom he has temporarily put in charge whilst he leaves his city. However, the Duke has not left Vienna and has secretly disguised himself as a friar to observe how Angelo and the city behave when he is absent. In this extract, the trick is an attempt to interfere with Angelo's rule, to save the brother of Isabella whom Angelo has condemned to death for sex before marriage as the law dictates. To save Isabella's brother, the Duke sends Angelo the head of another man who has just died. (Reasons for the Duke's trick, his absence and Angelo's cruelty are complex but they involve hypocritical sexual morality and behaviour.) Isabella arrives to ask if her brother has been pardoned and saved.

DUKE
Quick, dispatch, and send the head to Angelo.

Exit Provost

Now will I write letters to Varrius –
The provost, he shall bear them – whose contents
Shall witness to him I am near at home,
And by that great injunctions I am bound
To enter publicly. Him I'll desire
To meet me at the consecrated fount

A league below the city, and from thence,
By cold gradation and well-balanced form,
We shall proceed with Angelo.

Enter Provost

PROVOST
Here is the head. I'll carry it myself.

DUKE
Convenient is it. Make a swift return,
For I would commune with you of such things
That want no ears but yours.
PROVOST   I'll make all speed. *Exit.*

ISABELLA (*within*)
Peace, ho, be here.

DUKE
The tongue of Isabel. She's come to know
If yet her brother's pardon be come hither,
But I will keep her ignorant of her good,
To make her heavenly comforts of despair
When it is least expected.

Enter Isabella

ISABELLA   Ho, by your leave!

DUKE
Good morning to you, fair and gracious daughter.

ISABELLA
That better, given me by so holy a man.
Hath yet the deputy sent my brother's pardon?

DUKE
He hath released him, Isabel, from the world.
His head is off and sent to Angelo.

Measure for Measure by William Shakespeare (1604).
Act 4, Scene 3, lines 90–114

Summary

In this chapter, you have examined how actors and acting are important contexts in the construction of text and performance in Elizabethan and Jacobean drama. You have considered the significance of:

- the reputation of actors
- the use of boy players
- acting styles
- dramatic techniques
- 'actors and acting' in text and context.

10 Settings

The dramatic importance of setting

Most information on setting in plays from this period is conveyed to the audience through language with a minimal use of props. Let us explore the range of settings you might find.

Multiple settings

There may be multiple settings in your play/s. Firstly, there will be an overall place or location of the play; for example a country, geographical region or city. This might be referred to within the play, either in the stage directions or by the characters, or it might be part of the background information for actors and audiences without being named in the play.

The function of settings

Within that overall location, there might be more specific locations. For example, a house, a country estate, a palace or castle, a court building, an inn, a convent or church, a market square, a forest, a battlefield. Within that specific location, there might be further named locations. For example, in indoor settings, a significant room that is associated with particular activities. Rooms can have a significant dramatic function – domestic, personal or sexual, social, occupational, legal, political or religious.

The dramatic use of setting

Let us explore the dramatic use of setting in your plays.

- Are there any significant, named shifts between settings in your plays? Where, when and why do they take place?

- Do your settings shift in layers? For example, from the overall to the detailed, as outlined above? Do they shift from one overall setting to another – for example, from city to city or country to country? How do these shifts contribute to the structure and plot in your play?

- Are there dual settings? For example, two main locations with equal importance in the play. What is the significance of any dual settings? For example, town and country in a comedy.

- Are the settings outdoors or indoors? Are outdoor settings controlled by society or nature?

- What is the significance of the physical spaces or environments? The weather and climate? How do they develop the mood of the play or scene? How is language used to convey any significant relationships between mood, environment and weather in the play?

- How does the setting and any shift/s develop the plot, themes and characterisation in the play? For example, if a play has a trial plot-line of an 'accused' character – to discuss ideas about justice and the law – how does setting affect the reception of those ideas? For example, Vittoria's arraignment in *The White Devil*, the punishment of Angelo and charging of Lucio in *Measure for Measure*, the sentencing of Volpone and Mosca.

- Setting is important to dramatic structure. What is the structural significance of the shift/s in your play/s? How does genre affect the structural use of setting in your play/s?

- Are the settings geographical or/and symbolic? Does it matter where it is or/and what it represents?

- How does the use of locations in your play/s show you any Elizabethan or Jacobean contexts?

Let us explore the contextual significance of these settings below.

The locations of plays

Let us consider the contextual significance of setting a play in England, in a world apart/outside England or in a natural landscape.

In England
A rare event
Of the plays we cover from this period, few are set in England and even fewer name a city or region. Fewer still are the ones set in the contemporary world of the Elizabethan and Jacobean societies. The Elizabethan plays that you might study with an identifiable English setting are those where it is impossible to do anything else: the English histories of Shakespeare and Marlowe. Set in the historical past, their plot-lines do not directly present any contemporary Elizabethan and Jacobean history.

The only Jacobean tragedy set in England that you might study is Shakespeare's *King Lear*. Like the histories, it is set in a distant past, notionally Ancient Britain. The play's setting presents a very different England to that of Shakespeare and his contemporaries. *Macbeth* is set in medieval Scotland. Written around the time of the Gunpowder Plot (1605), the setting of this play is in the context of James I's accession to the English throne.

Is this England?
There are very few Elizabethan comedies set in England. Shakespeare's *As You Like It* is mostly set in the Forest of Arden but Arden has multiple geographical possibilities: the area near Stratford, the French Ardennes, a classical combination of the Greek Arcadia (also meaning Heaven) and the Garden of Eden. The location remains unsettled and it is argued that the forest world in the play is symbolic: a fantasy setting of no geographical significance. The contextual significance of setting in this play lies elsewhere. If you study the play, consider the questions on 'The dramatic use of setting' given previously (page 86), and refer to the section 'Controlling nature' later in this chapter (page 89).

What is interesting is that wherever they are set, Shakespearian plays are populated with the images of the English countryside, from shepherds to indigenous flowers and plants. For example, in *Hamlet* and *As You Like It*.

Did you know?

The subversion of settings
Elizabethan and Jacobean dramatists often subvert the use of a setting. Events and action can happen in locations that you do not expect or associate with their usual functions. For example: young women and dukes thrown on foreign shores in *Twelfth Night* and *The Tempest*, fugitive nobles sheltering in a forest instead of a palace in *As You Like It*, senior church officials in bedrooms with married – or any – women in *The White Devil*.

What is significiant about subverting a setting?

Examiner's tip

The contextual significance of setting
Focus on **why** the dramatist has used a setting – select the relevant contexts affecting their use. Consider the effects of setting on dramatic language and structure of your play/s.

Do not describe the setting, or focus on the geographical location or the history of a place, or assert knowledge of that place – this factual information is **always** irrelevant to the question.

City comedy

The London city comedy of the Jacobean era foregrounds contemporary English settings, such as Jonson's satirical play, *The Alchemist* which is set in its contemporary London. Jonson wants to comment critically on attitudes and behaviour of Jacobean Londoners so stages the drama explicitly in that time and place. However, he chooses differently in *Volpone*, as you can see in 'The Italian setting' later in this chapter (page 90).

A world apart

Nowhere like home

Setting a play outside England was very popular in this period. It attracted every playwright in every genre. Why do you think that is? The Italian connection was so popular it has its own section later in this chapter. Let us consider the contextual significance of the Elizabethan and Jacobean appetite for plays set beyond England's shores.

Settings that present a world apart from the dominant social structures of the world in the play have dramatic significance for the exploration of themes and ideas. Why do you think the dramatist removes the characters from their everyday world in the play to put them in an unfamiliar environment? Why not present them dealing with situations and relationships in the familiar setting of their home environments? How does your play use a 'world apart'?

Classical and Mediterranean settings

Elizabethan and Jacobean dramatists use two significant settings outside of England and Italy: the classical world, of a Mediterranean past centred on Ancient Greece and Rome, and the region we now call Europe. The exception is Shakespeare's last play, *The Tempest*, set on an unnamed, possibly Caribbean, island.

Shakespeare

In the drama of this period, most of Shakespeare's ancient and tragic histories are set in the classical world. For example, the Roman Empire in *Antony and Cleopatra*, *Titus Andronicus* and *Coriolanus*, the Greek world in *Troilus and Cressida*. Shakespearian comedy also uses the classical world as a location. For example, *A Midsummer Night's Dream* is set in Athens in an unspecified time.

The setting of Illyria in *Twelfth Night* signifies a vaguely traced journey between somewhere Italian and the Turkish Mediterranean. The heroine is washed onto the shore after a shipwreck into a world of pirates and the sea. Despite this, Shakespeare presents the town and streets of Illyria the way that Elizabethan London would have looked.

Mainland European settings

The plays you might study that use mainland European settings outside of Italy are by Kyd, Marlowe and Shakespeare. The Kyd and Marlowe plays are Elizabethan. The Shakespeare plays are both Elizabethan and Jacobean. The plots include journeys across countries in what we now call Europe.

Think about it

Setting and contemporary commentary

How do dramatists use a foreign setting to make contemporary points about Elizabethan or Jacobean society?

Links

For more information, see Chapter 4, 'The Renaissance context': 'The interest in foreign travel' (page 30); 'The influence of classical ideals' (page 26).

Did you know?

The Spanish Tragedy

This play belongs with the plays set in Italy. It shares their mood and the contemporary attitudes that present Italy as a corrupt and evil enemy of England.

Did you know?

Measure for Measure

Shakespeare presents the city of Vienna as a seedy den of sexual sleaze and crime. It would have seemed, to Jacobean Londoners, like the world of their own contemporary theatre... (There is evidence that it was originally scripted with an Italian setting.)

Journeys

Journeys take place on and off stage in the plays or form the back story of the plot in the opening setting. They often involve trickery. For example, Marlowe's *Doctor Faustus* is set in Germany and shifts to Rome to mock the Pope with magic tricks. *Hamlet* is set in Denmark and references Poland, is threatened by Norway and travels to England. The first two countries involve war and territory and the final journey is used to show how Hamlet cannot be tricked. *Measure for Measure* is set in the city of Vienna (in modern Austria). The central character of the Duke pretends to travel outside the city to an unspecified place but remains in disguise to spy on his subjects and deputy.

Activity 1

Settings and journeys outside England

- Consider the plays discussed in this chapter. Refer back to Chapter 4 (page 26). How do the dramatists use a setting or journey outside England?

- How are the political and social contexts of the Renaissance significant in the settings of those plays?

- Consider your own play/s. How are Renaissance contexts important in their use of setting?

A forest setting in *A Midsummer Night's Dream*

Wild landscapes

The use of a wild landscape such as woodland, forest, heath or a remote island is symbolically significant in Shakespeare's Elizabethan and Jacobean drama. A woodland or forest setting in a comedy can symbolise escape from reality for the characters. A heath in a tragedy can suggest hostility or danger.

Controlling nature

A controlled natural setting such as a park, tended grounds of a country estate, a garden or a water feature is significant in Shakespearian drama. In a garden, characters can take a breather from the ordered life of its house, from prying eyes or even their own thoughts. The role of a controlled natural setting might be to clarify their thoughts. A garden can provide the setting for comic resolution within a fruitful or serene outcome and mood. It can create dramatic tension through benign deceptions. It might be the setting for lovers and comic subplots to chase around in a carefree fashion.

How's the weather doing?

The weather in plays from this period is significant. In all literature in any period, weather and its changes are often symbolic. Weather is used to reflect the mood of an episode or whole play. **Pathetic fallacy** is used to present the emotional states, fortunes and relationships of the characters.

In Elizabethan and Jacobean drama, thunder and lightning are used as a device to alert the audience to a supernatural setting or event. Storms and shipwrecks are traditional openings for romantic comedy and tragi-comedy and are used in this period to place characters in a world apart from their

---

Think about it

Natural settings

Consider how a natural setting is linked to the fortunes of the characters in the plot. Is nature presented as a supportive or a dangerous environment, or both, for each of the characters?

Links

For more information, see Chapter 11, 'The significance of indoor and outdoor spaces' (page 100) and Chapter 13, 'Chronology of events' (page 107).

Key term

Pathetic fallacy the use of weather and landscape to reflect or symbolise human emotions.

home. The sea is used as a setting where catastrophic weather temporarily separates important characters from each other. In a comedy, harmonious weather re-unites them.

Commonly in revenge tragedy, very hot weather or references to heat and overheating symbolise a character's passions of desire or anger. Every type of weather can be dangerous in Elizabethan and Jacobean tragedy. Sunshine and warmth in comedy usually symbolise harmony or love within an innocent or pleasurable situation.

What time is it?
Weather can be linked to the season and time of year. If the weather is presented as unexpected, unusual or extreme, there might be underhand or alarming plot developments in your play and an unsafe setting for the characters this affects.

At what time of day or night do events happen in your play/s? The cover of darkness and the dawning of a new day have symbolic significance in your play/s. What is interesting is the way in which darkness would have been differently conveyed in indoor and outdoor theatres. The date of composition affects this as the move to indoor theatre was widespread in the Jacobean era. Check when and where your play was originally performed.

The dramatic significance of Italy
The Italian setting
Italian settings dominate Elizabethan and Jacobean drama. Every playwright used an Italian setting. The Jacobean revenge tragedies you might study by Middleton, Webster and Ford are set in Italy. Marlowe wrote tragedies set in Italy and Shakespeare wrote plays set in Italy across the genres. Jonson's satirical city comedy, *Volpone*, is set in Venice.

The role of Italy
Elizabethan England's acceptance of Protestantism and rejection of Roman Catholicism had a major contextual impact on the drama. Presentations of a corrupt Italy were popular during this period. Themes and ideas exploited contemporary beliefs of Italian evil and moral degradation in plot-lines and characterisations. You can explore this in the tragedies of *Doctor Faustus*, *The Revenger's Tragedy*, *The Duchess of Malfi*, *The White Devil* and *'Tis Pity She's a Whore*. Apart from Marlowe's play, these Jacobean revenge tragedies were not only set in Italy but, as you know, also used features of Seneca's model of revenge tragedy (Seneca was himself a Roman).

Venice
The setting of Venice is used in plays by Shakespeare and Jonson to present a materialistic, greedy merchant-culture based on sea-trading and usury (money-lending).

The advantage of distance
The use of corrupt Italy as a setting could prove useful if a dramatist wanted to criticise society and behaviour in contemporary England, especially London. Italian settings offered a scapegoat. It was far enough away to be a safe criticism – no English Elizabethan or Jacobean playwright would be

A typical Italian palace and courtyard setting

executed for their portrayal of the Catholic Church and its officials, the Italian aristocracy or their merchants, never mind Italian Jews; near enough for the presentation to be credible, based on Renaissance beliefs and attitudes to Italy.

Jonson, however, was not shy of social criticism – he wrote satires. He openly criticised greed, vice, the worship of empty, soulless material idols and the trade in extracting money from others.

The dramatic use of travel and exotica

Elizabethan and Jacobean drama presents ideas about travel, exotic people, landscapes and places that reflect the contemporary contexts. Places and peoples whose language, society, race and nationality – their cultures – were different from the dominant cultural English models are presented as symbols of the unknown.

The Renaissance and the unknown

As you know, Elizabethan and Jacobean England was not a democracy. You also know that the social and legal position of English women – despite a powerful queen – and the working classes was unequal to that of men and the aristocracy. The 16th- and 17th-century English attitude of the ruling class towards the unknown was to give it the same low social status as they accorded English women and the working classes. These attitudes were supported by the Church. People from places remote from England are represented as something 'other' in drama of the period. At best they are presented as servants. At worst, monstrous or dangerous, even if their social status is more favourable. Consequently, an exotic setting is not only a world apart, it symbolises fear, danger and the uncivilised world – like a wild, natural setting, but more intensely so.

Stereotypes of the exotic

We know from references in tragedies such as Shakespeare's *Othello* that racism already existed. The word, colour and skin tone of 'black' was part of that 'other', the world apart, and is presented as something to be feared. Stereotypes of sexually lascivious, aggressive and animalistic natives and their untamed wilderness homes became embedded in the Elizabethan and Jacobean English ideology. The history of colonisation and slavery, in which England later became a key player, supports this idea.

These political and social contexts shaped some of the literature. A distant island setting reflects some engagement with racist presentations of a place and its inhabitants. The characterisation of Caliban in *The Tempest* is a complex example and attracts fierce debate for its ambivalent presentations of the 'other' in the play.

Attraction to the exotic

However, the trade routes and navigational achievements of Elizabethan and Jacobean maritime England opened up a world that was previously unimaginable to the English. Strange and unusual places and societies encountered by merchants and navies would have appeared exciting

---

Links

For more information, see Chapter 8, 'Significant character types in context': 'Rulers' (page 66); 'Church officials and religious figures' (page 69) and Chapter 5, 'Tragedy': 'What the Romans did for us' (page 37).

Think about it

Usury in Venice

Venice was rich from shipping cargo. The Jews of the city were restricted by law to the trade of usury. Christians could not practise usury by law as it was deemed an unchristian act of profiteering. However, as merchants, they wanted credit to profit from investment in shipping ventures – hence Shylock and *The Merchant of Venice*.

Christians, Jews, the English and the Italians

Consider who is presented as greedy, materialistic or corrupt in your plays. How does this show you the Elizabethan and Jacobean political and social contexts of your play/s?

An exotic wilderness setting, typical of *The Tempest*

and marvellous. A tropical island with turquoise waterfalls and luscious vegetation must have seemed fantastical to a rain-soaked sailor from Southampton.

The world was not yet fully charted. Everything was new for the English traveller. They knew there could be more compelling exotica over the horizon. Imagine a time when a potato and tobacco were the height of foreign glamour and you can begin to understand the attraction.

Exotic settings in the drama

This tension of attraction and repulsion with exotica – based on a mixture of ignorance, innocence and a self-imposed superiority – did not escape the dramatists. This complex relationship between England and what was dubbed 'The New World' is explored in Shakespeare's play, *The Tempest*.

Webster characterises the foreign peoples of his plays (namely Moors) in an Italian setting, of which you know the significance. You can guess that things do not end well for these characters. Webster presents the social hardships for young black female and male servants in the cut-throat society of a corrupt court in *The White Devil*, severed from an environment where their social position might have been very different.

> ### Link
>
> For more information, see Chapter 4, 'The Renaissance context': 'The interest in foreign travel' (page 30).

How to contextualise the settings in your play

> ### Applying context questions 1
>
> **Settings in context**
> Read the three extracts below. They are from early in the plays.
>
> 1. For each extract, analyse how setting is presented. How is it used to introduce plot, theme and character? Analyse how the context of reception influences your response to each extract.
>
> 2. Compare and contrast the use of settings across the three extracts.
>
> 3. How are the literary, social and political contexts of these plays revealed in the extracts?
>
> 4. Consider your own plays. Select an extract of 20–50 lines in which the setting is dramatically significant. Analyse how the language depicts your setting. How does the setting show you the literary, social and political contexts of your play?

Extract 1

William Shakespeare, *As You Like It*

The play is a pastoral romantic comedy. The extract is from early in the play. The Duke, his attendant Amiens and other loyal Lords have been wrongly exiled from the royal court. They take refuge and shelter in the forest where they attempt to resolve the practical, social and political problems of injustice they now face. The disguises help them look as if they belong in the forest.

Enter DUKE SENIOR, AMIENS, *and two or three* LORDS *dressed as foresters*

DUKE SENIOR
Now, my co-mates and brothers in exile,
Hath not old custom made this life more sweet
Than that of painted pomp? Are not these woods
More free from peril than the envious court?
Here feel we not the penalty of Adam,
The seasons' difference, as the icy fang
And churlish chiding of the winter's wind –
Which when it bites and blows upon my body
Even till I shrink with cold, I smile and say,
'This is no flattery' – these are counsellors
That feelingly persuade me what I am.
Sweet are the uses of adversity
Which like the toad, ugly and venomous,
Wears yet a precious jewel in his head,
And this our life exempt from public haunt
Finds tongues in trees, books in the running brooks,
Sermons in stones, and good in everything.

AMIENS
I would not change it; happy is your grace
That can translate the stubbornness of Fortune
Into so quiet and so sweet a style.

DUKE SENIOR
Come, shall we go and kill us venison?
And yet it irks me the poor dappled fools,
Being native burghers of this desert city,
Should, in their own confines, with forked heads
Have their round haunches gored.

As You Like It by William Shakespeare (1599).
Act 2, Scene 1, lines 1–24

Extract 2
John Webster, *The Duchess of Malfi*

The play is a later Jacobean revenge tragedy. The extract is the opening lines of the play. Antonio is the steward at Malfi's royal court. Returning from his travels, he praises the French system of governing a palace in contrast with Malfi. Delio is Antonio's friend. Bosola is the malcontent, a servant to the corrupt Cardinal. The Cardinal is the Duchess of Malfi's brother and with Bosola will plot her downfall. Antonio becomes the secret husband of the Duchess.

[*Enter* ANTONIO *and* DELIO]

DELIO
You are welcome to your country, dear Antonio;
You have been very long in France, and you return
A very formal Frenchman in your habit.
How do you like the French court?

ANTONIO   I admire it:
In seeking to reduce both state and people
To a fixed order, their judicious king
Begins at home, quits first his royal palace
Of flatt'rng sycophants, of dissolute
And infamous persons – which he sweetly terms
His Master's masterpiece, the work of heaven –
Consid'ring duly that a prince's court
Is like a common fountain, whence should flow
Pure silver drops in general, but if't chance
Some cursed example poison't near the head,
Death and diseases through the whole land spread.
And what is't makes this blessed government
But a most provident council, who dare freely
Inform him the corruption of the times?
Though some o'th court hold it presumption
To instruct princes what they ought to do,
It is a noble duty to inform them
What they ought to foresee.

[*Enter* BOSOLA]

                              Here comes Bosola,
The only court-gall; yet I observe his railing
Is not for simple love of piety,
Indeed he rails at those things which he wants,
Would be as lecherous, covetous, or proud,
Bloody, or envious, as any man,
If he had means to be so.

[*Enter* CARDINAL]

                              Here's the Cardinal.

The Duchess of Malfi by John Webster (1612).
Act 1, Scene 1, lines 1–28

Extract 3
William Shakespeare, *The Tempest*

The play is a tragi-comedy. The extract is from the second scene of the play. Formerly the Duke of Milan, Prospero is the ruler of the island. The back story of the play is that he arrived in a small boat with his baby daughter, now a young woman, after being usurped by his ambitious brother in Milan by the King of Naples. Prospero has since learned magic. He creates a storm at the beginning of the play, the tempest, which shipwrecks the King, his son and men onto the island. Prospero has also used magic, wielded by his servant, the supernatural spirit Ariel, to threaten and enslave Caliban. Caliban is the only surviving original inhabitant of the island. Sycorax, Caliban's mother, now dead, had previously enslaved Ariel. Caliban has also tried to rape Prospero's daughter.

PROSPERO
Thou poisonous slave, got by the devil himself
Upon thy wicked dam, come forth.
       Enter CALIBAN

CALIBAN
As wicked dew as e'er my mother brushed
With raven's feather from unwholesome fen
Drop on you both! A south-west blow on ye,
And blister you all o'er!

PROSPERO
For this, be sure, tonight thou shalt have cramps,
Side-stitches that shall pen thy breath up; urchins
Shall, for that vast of night that they may work,
All exercise on thee; thou shalt be pinched

As thick as honeycomb, each pinch more stinging
Than bees that made 'em.

CALIBAN   I must eat my dinner.
This island's mine by Sycorax my mother,
Which thou tak'st from me. When thou cam'st first
Thou strok'st me and made much of me; wouldst give me
Water with berries in't, and teach me how
To name the bigger light, and how the less,
That burn by day and night. And then I loved thee
And showed thee all the qualities o'th'isle,
The fresh springs, brine-pits, barren place and fertile –
Cursed be I that did so! All the charms
Of Sycorax – toads, beetles, bats – light on you!
For I am all the subjects that you have,
Which first was mine own king; and here you sty me
In this hard rock, whiles you do keep from me
The rest o'th'island.

PROSPERO   Thou most lying slave,
Whom stripes may move, not kindness! I have used thee,
Filth as thou art, with humane care, and lodged thee
In mine own cell, till thou didst seek to violate
The honour of my child.

CALIBAN   O ho, O ho! Would't had been done.
Thou didst prevent me – I had peopled else
This isle with Calibans.

The Tempest by William Shakespeare (1611).
Act 1, Scene 2, lines 320–351

Summary

In this chapter, you have examined how setting is constructed in the contexts of Elizabethan and Jacobean drama. You have considered:

- the dramatic importance of setting
- the locations of plays of the period
- the dramatic significance of Italy
- the dramatic use of travel and exotica
- how to contextualise the settings in your play.

You now have a thorough grasp of how Elizabethan and Jacobean contexts influence the construction of each aspect of your plays. For additional historical contextual information, turn to Section C (page 96).

Theatre locations

You will find the location of each of the theatres on the map.

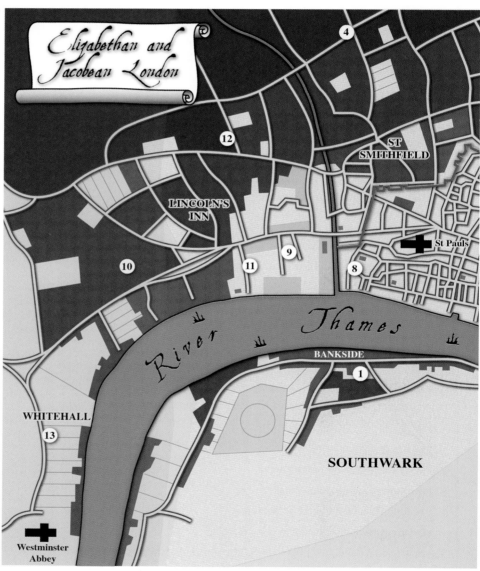

Elizabethan and Jacobean theatre locations in the City of London

Chapter aims

In this chapter, you will find information on:

- theatre locations
- the significance of indoor and outdoor spaces
- the patronage of theatre companies
- the Master of Revels.

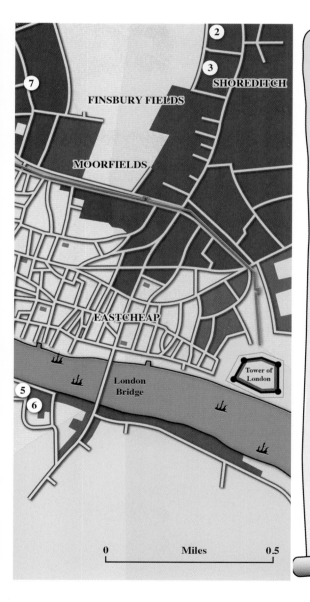

Theatres in London

1. The Swan
2. The Theatre
3. The Curtain
4. The Red Bull
5. The Rose
6. The Globe
7. The Fortune
8. Blackfriars Playhouse
9. Whitefriars Theatre Playhouse
10. The Cockpit
11. Middle Temple Inn Theatre Playhouse
12. Gray's Inn
13. The Whitehall Playhouse Theatre

Amphitheatres (outdoor)

1 **The Swan** (1574–): the largest, 3,000 spectators, also used for bear-baiting. Pembroke's Men were billed to be the first company to perform here but scandal and wrangle wrecked their contract.

2 **The Theatre** (1576–1597): the first purpose-built theatre built by James Burbage, in Shoreditch, north of the river. Burbage lost the lease so his acting company, Chamberlain's Men, dismantled it by night and used the timber to build the first Globe.

3 **The Curtain** (1577–1622): near the Theatre. Shakespeare and his early theatre company, Chamberlain's Men, performed here whilst waiting for the Globe to be built.

4 **The Red Bull** (1577–1665): the rowdiest. An inn-yard converted into a theatre in 1604. Queen Anne's Men (formerly Worcester's Men) were the first theatre company to perform here.

5 **The Rose** (1587–1606): the first purpose-built theatre on Bankside, south of the river. Edward Alleyn and his theatre company Lord Admiral's Men were based here, until they moved to the new Fortune Theatre. At the Rose, Alleyn played most of Marlowe's major characters.

6 **The Globe** (1599–1613; 1614–1642): situated on Bankside. The Globe belonged to actors who also owned the theatre company, Chamberlain's Men (to become Lord Chamberlain's Men). The Burbage brothers, Richard and Cuthbert, had double shares, Shakespeare had single shares. Shakespeare's company used it in the summer and performed at Blackfriars Theatre in the winter.

7 **The Fortune** (1600–1642): built by Edward Alleyn and his theatrical partner, father-in-law Philip Henslowe, on profits from the Rose Theatre. Designed to compete with the Globe, north of the City boundary.

Playhouses (indoor)

8 **Blackfriars Playhouse** (1576–1584; 1600–1642): associated with Shakespeare and the Burbages. From 1608, they used it in winter with their theatre company, The King's Men (formerly Lord Admiral's Men). Blackfriars was converted from a dissolved Dominican monastery.

9 **Whitefriars Theatre Playhouse** (1606–1629): the rectory hall of a priory converted into a theatre following the success of the Blackfriars.

10 **The Cockpit** (1609–1617; 1618–1649): re-named **The Phoenix** on reopening after a mob had burnt down the first. Originally a pit for cock fights and converted into a theatre in 1616 by Christopher Beeston, actor and leader of the theatre company, Beeston's Boys. Staged illicit plays after 1642 until discovered and closed down by Puritans.

11 **Middle Temple Inn Theatre Playhouse**: not a theatre as such, one of the Inns of Court, School of Law. The Great Hall was built in Elizabeth I's reign and used to put on plays in a lavish manner and setting. Shakespeare and his acting company at that time, now the Lord Chamberlain's Men, performed *Twelfth Night* there in 1602.

12 **Gray's Inn**. Like the Middle Temple Inn, an Inn of Court, School of Law with a Great Hall. The School of Law was attended by sons of the aristocracy and noblemen – for example, Sir Walter Raleigh – who had to stay in and watch plays at night. The Queen was the Gray's Inn patron.

13 **The Whitehall Playhouse Theatre**: designed by the famous architect, Inigo Jones, it was intended to be luxurious. Frequented by Elizabeth I.
Shakespeare and the Lord Chamberlain's Men played here, including after they had narrowly escaped punishment for staging a performance of *Richard II* the night before the Essex Rebellion.

The significance of the City boundary

The map details the locations of Elizabethan and Jacobean theatres. Out of all the important theatres that existed at the time, only Blackfriars Theatre and a handful of what were called the Elizabethan Inn Yards (because they were exactly that: the yard outside an inn that staged plays) are within the boundaries of the City of London, under the jurisdiction of the City, its Lord Mayor and the Corporation of London. The rest are outside of that jurisdiction.

The move to purpose-built theatres

In 1574, during the Elizabethan era, the authorities of the City of London started regulating what went on in the inn-yards and the putting-on of plays and players was frowned upon. Entrepreneurial actors and theatrical families who made a livelihood from the theatre, and private funders who invested in the theatre business, saw themselves being squeezed out of their profession within the City. As a result, they moved to pastures new, outside of the City's boundary. A theatre could be built cheaply in as little as six months, often involving the actors themselves in its construction and most certainly in the creation of the stage area. From 1574, huge amphitheatres that could seat and stand up to 3,000 people outdoors started to spring up all around the outside of the City boundary to add to the bear, bull and cockpits which existed already.

The other places that the City attempted to regulate were the pits and rings used for baiting bears and bulls, a popular Elizabethan and Jacobean pastime and spectator sport. These arenas were ideal for the early Elizabethan theatre – but by 1591, the beginning of the period we have considered, the popularity of theatre was compromising the bear and bull-baiting commercial schedule. The Bull Ring amphitheatre had to ban theatre on Thursdays so that the bear- and bull-baiting events could be put on in their own venues. (These blood-sports were not banned until 1835. When the Puritans closed the theatres in 1642, they allowed the bears and bulls to continue to be baited, so those venues stayed open.)

Conversions of inns and pits

Some inn-yards were later converted for theatrical use. The Red Bull is a famous example, where Webster's play *The White Devil* was staged. Some pits were converted into theatres, such as The Cockpit (to The Phoenix) and The Bear Garden (albeit temporarily, to The Hope). However, all these conversions did not take place until the Jacobean era and none was within the City boundaries.

Temporary theatre closures

Theatres were regularly being closed, temporarily, throughout the Elizabethan and Jacobean period, long before the Puritan ruling and the City's disapproval. Fire, food riots, mob attacks and the plague all halted performance, making the acting life a strain at times.

The significance of indoor and outdoor spaces

In the list of theatres on page 98, you can see which were indoor and which were outdoor venues for theatre performances. On the map you can see where each space was in relation to the others and to the City boundary.

Outdoor spaces

Accessibility

The most significant feature of the outdoor theatre space was its accessibility to all the social classes and everyone's pocket. The term 'box office' comes from the box into which the Elizabethans put their entrance penny for the cheapest spot, the box was then put in the office. The accessibility of the theatre was achieved through a huge space in which the groundlings stood on a dirt floor, exposed to the elements, and in which the wealthy sat, in varying degrees of comfort, under cover. The seats were more expensive the higher they were placed as the distance increased from the stink of the groundlings.

Physical space

The building was circular or octagonal. Stages were often temporary, jutting out into the standing audience and secured by pillars. Scenery and props were minimal and basic. Gambling was common on the ground. Toilets were non-existent. You went outside and then the sewage was buried or tipped into the River Thames.

Theatrical experience

Lighting was natural and plays were usually staged in the afternoon. To indicate night scenes and moods, the dialogue often indicated to the audience that it was dark. Artificial lighting of a lantern or a torch was often used to suggest the illusion of darkness. Special effects were limited to ropes for flying about the stage. Music came later. People chatted and interacted with the play – it would have been noisy.

Indoor spaces

Accessibility

The development of indoor spaces in the Elizabethan and Jacobean period, with specially built or converted theatres, paved the way for the modern theatre space as we know it today. The first difference to observe is its differentiated accessibility. No groundlings could afford to attend these spaces. The Great Halls of lavish buildings had existed in Elizabeth I's reign and put on plays for the elite but the indoor playhouse became a new phenomenon for people who were wealthy but not necessarily the aristocratic or noble elite.

Physical space

Indoor spaces were permanent, roofed, smaller, seated and comfortable – so it was more expensive to put on a play than in an an outdoor space would cost. Each audience member had to pay more – sometimes 26 times more. The more comfortable the seat, the more it cost.

Theatrical experience

As a theatre experience, there were some significant differences. It was quieter – there was no gambling, moving about or nipping outside to the toilet. Stage visibility and watching the events closely was more achievable. Careful listening to lines and speeches had a purpose as they could perhaps be expressed with more delicacy or subtlety in the acoustics of a more intimate, indoor space.

Lighting could be controlled indoors. Night productions became possible. The space was lit by candles, trimmed and replaced in the intervals between acts. You could buy refreshments during these times. The warmth permitted winter performances. Scenery could be left up, becoming ever more intricate. Music was used and designed to be heard as part of the play. Costumes became extravagant, protected from the rough and tumble of the outdoor stage. Sound and light/dark effects began to be introduced.

The patronage of theatre companies
The Vagabonds Act, 1572

The Act for the punishment of vagabonds – jugglers, pedlars and tinkers – added the category 'Common Players in Interludes' to its list of undesirables. When Parliament passed this Act, it classified actors as part of the 'Rogues, Vagabonds and Sturdy Beggars'. Actors had effectively been criminalised – unless they were part of a theatre company who happened to have the protection of a powerful and wealthy aristocrat such as a lord or baron. This person would act as the patron of the theatre company and vouch for an actor's respectability. As an actor, staying on the right side of your patron meant you had a living and avoided a whipping or getting your ears branded. This system lasted until the Act was updated in 1597 to reduce the punishment for being an actor. An actor still had to be licensed and only a great noble could give out these licences.

Theatre companies
Names of the companies

The Elizabethan and Jacobean theatre companies, to which the famous actors like Shakespeare, Richard Burbage and Edward Alleyn belonged, were under the patronage of a nobleman. The companies were named after their patron. Elizabeth I had been the patron for an earlier Elizabethan company called Queen Elizabeth's Men, whom she had ordered to form, but the rest of the theatre companies who had formed themselves were under the patronage of their particular noble.

Royal patronage

Once James I ascended to the English throne in 1603, he changed the system so that theatre companies had exclusively royal patronage. Their new names reflected those of the members of the immediate royal family to whom they belonged.

Performances at court

During the Elizabethan and Jacobean period, acting companies were invited, or commanded, to go to the royal court and perform for the entertainment of the royal family and their courtiers. Their patronage did not affect this – when the queen or king called, you went.

Significant theatre companies after 1590

- **Lord Chamberlain's Men**. Also known earlier as Chamberlain's Men (before he became Lord Chamberlain). This is the company which Shakespeare was with all his acting life and was one of the two greatest acting troupes of the period. The famous Burbage family were Lord Chamberlain's Men. The company enjoyed a significant level of protection from their patron, especially once he became the Lord Chamberlain, the most useful peer at Court, as he organised the court revels – and the powerful Master of Revels reported to him. The company held exclusive rights to perform Shakespeare's plays. In 1603, they became known as the **King's Players**, or the **King's Men**. When King James became James I of England, he became their patron. Additionally, Henry Wriothesley was the patron of William Shakespeare and his patronage bore a strong influence on the success of Shakespeare.

- **Lord Admiral's Men**. Also known earlier as Admiral's Men (before he became Lord Admiral). This is the other theatre company with the most significance in this period. In the Elizabethan era, there was some joint association with Lord Chamberlain's Men, such as acting together and sharing venues. This collaboration petered out as the competition between them grew. Edward Alleyn was their star actor. He played most of Marlowe's major characters. They gave the first performance of *Doctor Faustus* at the Rose theatre and then later at the Fortune.

- **Earl of Pembroke's Men**, despite performing Marlowe's *Edward II* and a handful of Shakespeare's plays, this was not a successful company, forged from a hotch-potch of the Lord Admiral's Men and the Lord Strange's Men.

- **Lord Strange's Men** did perform in London but were more often later found touring the provinces. Those who did not later join the Lord Admiral's Men formed a company called Derby's Men (after the Earl of Derby, the inherited title given to each Lord Strange) and played outside London.

- **Leicester's Men** were the first known theatre company in Elizabethan England but by 1590 they had merged with Lord Strange's Men.

- **Worcester's Men**. The Earl of Worcester wanted the prestige of an acting troupe in London. In the 1590s, the Lord Admiral's Men and the Lord Chamberlain's Men were the only two acting troupes of adult players of any note in London. They became licensed to play in London in 1602 and despite only being entitled to play at The Boar's Head, they started acting at the Rose when the Lord Admiral's Men moved to the Fortune. They joined with Oxford's Men to become **Queen Anne's Men** in the Jacobean era when James I's wife became their patron. At this time, they moved to the Red Bull and Christopher Beeston was their most important member.

- **Lady Elizabeth's Men**, or Princess Elizabeth's Men, had King James I's daughter Princess Elizabeth as their patron. From 1618, the company was renamed The Queen of Bohemia's Men, after Elizabeth and her husband unsuccessfully attempted to install themselves in Bohemia.

- **Queen Henrietta's Men**. This company was formed in 1625 at the start of the Caroline era by Christopher Beeston. They were named after their patron, the wife of Charles I. They were as popular as the long-established King's Men, Shakespeare and Burbage's company, and were the resident company at the Phoenix Theatre.

- **Children's companies.** Children's companies of boy actors were popular, either as the sole performers or merging with the adult companies as occasion dictated. Queen Elizabeth was especially fond of the children's companies. The companies were formed from choirs and churches or under the guidance of the owner of an acting company – for example, Christopher Beeston formed Beeston's Boys. Many of these companies performed at the Whitefriars Theatre.

Freedom from jurisdiction

The London theatre companies that were associated with a particular theatre that was outside of the city limits were known as 'the liberties' as they could perform plays that dealt with issues of which the Lord Mayor of the City did not approve. Eventually, in 1608, the authorities got their way and the City Charter dissolved the liberties, bringing all the out-of-boundary theatres under the authority of the City. It was too late, however, as James I already had them all under his immediate royal protection so the City elements of restraint were frustrated. This contributed to the growing Puritan resentment of all things royal – and theatrical.

The Master of Revels

The Master of Revels had a significant role to play in the theatre of Elizabeth and Jacobean London. He was the person who decided which plays would be performed at Court for royalty. He scheduled, invited and censored theatre companies and their plays according to his will. As well as pleasing the monarch, the troupe and the play had to please their own patron and then the Master of Revels. The Master of Revels could effectively bar, block or accelerate the fortunes of a theatre company or the plays of a contemporary playwright. The significance of being the Lord Chamberlain's Men is clear. As the Master of Revels reported to the Lord Chamberlain, having this patron strengthened the company's position and security significantly.

An Elizabethan acting company performs for the Queen

12 Key influences on tragedy and comedy

The Spanish Tragedy by Thomas Kyd
Popularity of Kyd's play

Kyd's play, first published in 1592 but believed to have been performed several years earlier, was consistently popular with theatre companies and audiences. There are records of extensive performances by companies including The Admiral's Men, Pembroke's Men and Lord Strange's Men. The play is referenced within other plays – known to contemporary actors and audiences by the name of its titular hero as 'Hieronimo's Play' – and discussed as dominating the stage in the plays of this period. Its influence cannot be overstated.

Dramatic significance
Genre

The Spanish Tragedy has been referenced throughout this book as the forerunner of Jacobean revenge tragedy, based on an adaptation of the conventions of Senecan tragedy and its influence upon the Elizabethan and Jacobean tragedy genre, in particular on revenge drama from this period.

Language

Kyd had a further influence on the drama of this period. He was an innovator in his use of the iambic pentameter verse within the language of the play. The emphasis on the iambic pentameter blank verse form is echoed by Marlowe's language use in his plays *Tamburlaine the Great* and *Doctor Faustus*. As Marlowe did later, Kyd blended the Senecan style with the medieval English conventions of the medieval morality play to deliver a drama that is more sophisticated than it might have sometimes been considered.

Despite the appearance of a straightforward revenge drama, Kyd's inventive language use and his selection of subgenre features to reach his contemporary audience combine to create a significant play within the period and one that repays a little familiarity. The plot is complex and requires some unpicking.

Plot summary

The plot features the story of the graphic and horrific annihilation of the heirs to the Spanish and Portuguese thrones through a complex and duplicitous series of revenge killings.

Structurally, the play is framed by a ghost story: the ghost of Don Andrea, a Spanish noble who fell dishonourably in battle with the Portuguese, seeks revenge. He wants to witness the murder of his enemies. The figure of Revenge, a traditional morality figure, promises him that he will have his revenge and its proof.

Don Andrea's principal enemy is his murderer, Balthazar: the heir of Portugal. Balthazar is imprisoned in Spain after he was captured in the same battle by Don Horatio, another Spanish noble. Don Horatio is Hieronimo's son. He becomes the lover of Andrea's former intended, Bel-Imperia. So

Andrea has a grudge against both Balthazar and Don Horatio, and Bel-Imperia for betrayal. Bel-Imperia is also the niece to the Spanish King, who has no children, so she is his heir. Before she can take her revenge on Balthazar for Andrea's death, her own brother Lorenzo helps Balthazar escape, murder Don Horatio and imprison Bel-Imperia to keep her quiet.

Hieronimo is mad with grief at the death of Horatio. He is driven further into a state of madness when he receives a letter from the trapped Bel-Imperia, telling him who murdered his son and written in her blood. He asks the King of Spain for justice; he does not continue the cycle of revenge killing. However, the King of Spain has arranged for the marriage of Balthazar to his niece to unite Spain and Portugal, end the wars and produce heirs for the Spanish throne. Hieronimo feels that he has had no justice for the crimes committed against him. Worse, his wife commits suicide in grief and he receives another letter telling him who murdered his son. Now he wants revenge.

Hieronimo debates the Stoic suffering of letting God take justice for his loss or avenging the murder and death of his family. He chooses vengeance. He plots with Bel-Imperia, who does not want to marry Balthazar, to stage a play-within-a-play for the Court, to catch and kill Lorenzo and Balthazar. During this enactment, Hieronimo kills Lorenzo and Bel-Imperia kills Balthazar and herself. The reality of what he has witnessed dawns on the King of Spain – the young characters who could be heirs are all dead before him.

Hieronimo reveals the corpse of his son as motive, then bites out his own tongue rather than give any information or apology to the King. The initial framing device returns: the ghost of Andrea and the morality figure of Revenge, triumphant in the revenge that Andrea has received from the deaths in the play.

Cast list – Dramatis Personae

GHOST OF ANDREA
REVENGE
KING OF SPAIN
CYPRIAN, DUKE OF CASTILE, *his brother*
LORENZO, *the Duke's son*
BEL-IMPERIA, *Lorenzo's sister*
GENERAL *of the Spanish army*

VICEROY OF PORTUGAL
PEDRO, *his brother*
BALTHAZAR, *his son*
ALEXANDRO}*Portuguese*
VILUPPIO } *noblemen*
AMBASSADOR *of Portugal*

HIERONIMO, *Knight Marshal of Spain*
ISABELLA, *his wife*
HORATIO, *their son*

PEDRINGANO, *servant to Bel-Imperia*
SERBERINE, *servant to Balthazar*
CHRISTOPHIL, *servant to Lorenzo*
BAZULTO, *an old man*

Page *to Lorenzo*, Three Watchmen, Messenger, Deputy, Hangman, Maid *to Isabella*, Two Portuguese, Servant, Three Citizens, Portuguese Nobles, Soldiers, Officers, Attendants, Halberdiers

Three Knights, Three Kings, a Drummer *in the first Dumb-show* Hymen, Two Torch-bearers *in the second Dumb-show*

Character types

Ruler: King of Spain
Tragic revenge hero: Hieronimo, who is also the character who **goes mad**
Villains: Balthazar and Lorenzo
Women: Bel-Imperia, feisty, courageous and assertive; Isabella, Hieronimo's wife who commits suicide in grief at her son's death
Working classes: servants; including Pedringano, servant to Castiza, who betrays her to Lorenzo
Supernatural figures: of a ghost and a morality figure

Commedia dell'arte
Origins and influences

Commedia dell'arte is a comic subgenre of drama that originates from the mid-16th century in Renaissance Italy when actors travelled around in troupes. The form has been very influential on European comedy, including the masque, and was much beloved by Jonson who adapted features of this into his satires. *Commedia* is classically influenced and also contains the conventions of both morality plays and farce.

Our name 'slapstick' comes from the tradition that one of the characters, Arlecchino, has a stock habit of banging two sticks together as part of a joke.

Genre

This is professional yet improvised comedy. It is built and structured around a pre-established scenario so that the drama is both disciplined and free-flowing at the same time.

Acting styles

Commedia dell'arte is a very physical form and features dynamic movement in which the characters jump and roll about, trading stock jokes, almost like a pantomime. Actors wear masks so they use their body to communicate feelings. Characters wear spectacular costumes and specific clothing, as well as using a particular style of language, to identify their character type. A jester, wearing the sparkly costume of a harlequin, was always present.

Performances were given on a makeshift stage, usually on the street but sometimes at royal courts. Sets and staging were minimalistic to allow for travelling and quick assembly in public outdoor spaces.

Character types

Arlecchino: the most famous: an acrobat and a sharp comedian in a cat-like mask.

Brighella: the villain. Arlecchino's dubious friend but more of a rogue. Slick and materialistic.

Il Capitano (the captain): a parody of a soldier but cowardly. Always Spanish.

Il Dottore (the doctor): a parody of scholarship and a con-man.

Pantalone: a parody of the Venetian merchant: a miserable, greedy, rich old man with a much younger wife or an adventurous daughter.

Pedrolino: a white-faced, moon-struck dreamer, much like our modern clowns.

Scarramuccia: dressed in black and brandishing a sword, the dashing hero.

Inamorato: the handsome lover who goes by many names. He is the only character without a mask and has to be silver-tongued for the love speeches.

Inamorata: the female lover. Her servant is the beloved of Harlequin.

Harlequin: a fast-moving clown who can be stupid but not outwitted. Greedy, loves the female servant.

La Ruffiana: an old woman, the mother, or a gossip, who scuppers the lovers.

Cantarina and Ballerina: their main role is to sing, dance or play music.

13 Chronology of events

THE ELIZABETHAN ERA

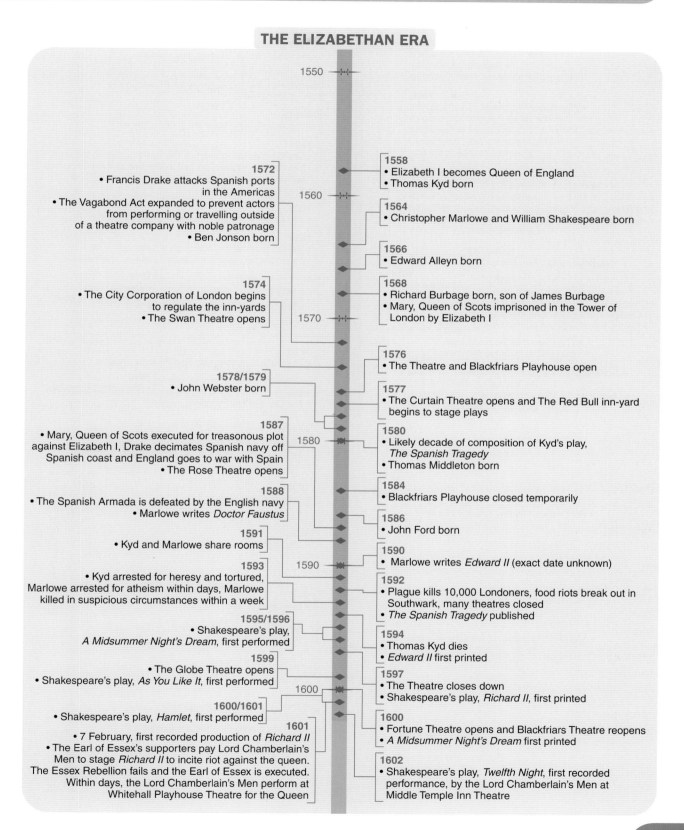

1550

1558
• Elizabeth I becomes Queen of England
• Thomas Kyd born

1560

1572
• Francis Drake attacks Spanish ports in the Americas
• The Vagabond Act expanded to prevent actors from performing or travelling outside of a theatre company with noble patronage
• Ben Jonson born

1564
• Christopher Marlowe and William Shakespeare born

1566
• Edward Alleyn born

1574
• The City Corporation of London begins to regulate the inn-yards
• The Swan Theatre opens

1568
• Richard Burbage born, son of James Burbage
• Mary, Queen of Scots imprisoned in the Tower of London by Elizabeth I

1570

1576
• The Theatre and Blackfriars Playhouse open

1578/1579
• John Webster born

1577
• The Curtain Theatre opens and The Red Bull inn-yard begins to stage plays

1587
• Mary, Queen of Scots executed for treasonous plot against Elizabeth I, Drake decimates Spanish navy off Spanish coast and England goes to war with Spain
• The Rose Theatre opens

1580

1580
• Likely decade of composition of Kyd's play, *The Spanish Tragedy*
• Thomas Middleton born

1588
• The Spanish Armada is defeated by the English navy
• Marlowe writes *Doctor Faustus*

1584
• Blackfriars Playhouse closed temporarily

1586
• John Ford born

1591
• Kyd and Marlowe share rooms

1590
• Marlowe writes *Edward II* (exact date unknown)

1590

1593
• Kyd arrested for heresy and tortured, Marlowe arrested for atheism within days, Marlowe killed in suspicious circumstances within a week

1592
• Plague kills 10,000 Londoners, food riots break out in Southwark, many theatres closed
• *The Spanish Tragedy* published

1595/1596
• Shakespeare's play, *A Midsummer Night's Dream*, first performed

1594
• Thomas Kyd dies
• *Edward II* first printed

1599
• The Globe Theatre opens
• Shakespeare's play, *As You Like It*, first performed

1597
• The Theatre closes down
• Shakespeare's play, *Richard II*, first printed

1600

1600/1601
• Shakespeare's play, *Hamlet*, first performed

1600
• Fortune Theatre opens and Blackfriars Theatre reopens
• *A Midsummer Night's Dream* first printed

1601
• 7 February, first recorded production of *Richard II*
• The Earl of Essex's supporters pay Lord Chamberlain's Men to stage *Richard II* to incite riot against the queen. The Essex Rebellion fails and the Earl of Essex is executed. Within days, the Lord Chamberlain's Men perform at Whitehall Playhouse Theatre for the Queen

1602
• Shakespeare's play, *Twelfth Night*, first recorded performance, by the Lord Chamberlain's Men at Middle Temple Inn Theatre

THE JACOBEAN ERA

1604
• James I becomes King of Great Britain, France and Ireland. Church uproar ensues
• *Doctor Faustus* A-text published
• Shakespeare's play, *Measure for Measure*, first performed

1600

1603
• James VI of Scotland becomes James I, King of England
• James I gives all London theatre companies royal patronage
• Shakespeare's play, *Hamlet*, first printed

1605
• Guy Fawkes and the Gunpowder Plotters try to blow up Parliament

1606
• Whitefriars Playhouse Theatre opens
• The Rose Theatre closes down
• Jonson's play, *Volpone*, first performed at the Globe
• Shakespeare's play, *King Lear*, first recorded performance

1605/1606
• Shakespeare's play, *Macbeth*, first performed

1608
• City Charter dissolves 'the liberties' to bring all theatres into the City jurisdiction, but ineffective as the companies are under royal patronage and too well-established
• *King Lear* first printed

1607
• Jamestown, Virginia is the first permanent settlement in North America
The Revenger's Tragedy first published (not attributed to an author until 1656) debate over the authorship of Middleton or Cyril Tourneur

1610

1609
• The Cockpit Theatre begins to stage plays

1610
• Galileo looks at stars through a telescope – his astronomical predictions seen as magic and heresy

1609/1612
• Webster writes *The White Devil*

1616
• William Shakespeare dies
• Christopher Beeston converts the Cockpit into a playhouse theatre
• *Doctor Faustus* B-text published

1614
• 2nd Globe opens

1612
• Webster writes *The Duchess of Malfi*

1613
• Globe Theatre burns down

1620
• The Pilgrim Fathers sail from England to colonise America

1620

1617
• The Cockpit Theatre is burnt down by a mob

1618
• The Cockpit reopens as The Phoenix Theatre

1623
• Shakespeare's First Folio published, including *As You Like It, Twelfth Night, Measure for Measure, Macbeth, The Tempest*
• *The Duchess of Malfi* first printed

1619
• Richard Burbage dies

1622
• The Curtain Theatre closes down

THE CAROLINE ERA

1625
• Charles I inherits the throne from his father James I to become King of England and Scotland

1627
• Thomas Middleton dies

1630

1630
• John Webster dies

1629/1633
• Ford writes *'Tis Pity She's a Whore*

1633
• *'Tis Pity She's a Whore* first printed

1637
• Ben Jonson dies

1639
• John Ford disappears from the records

1640

THE ENGLISH CIVIL WARS

1642
• The Caroline era ends and the Puritans assume power
• The remaining theatres are closed down by the Puritans until the Restoration in 1660

1649
• Charles I is executed. The Puritans rule England and her empire in the First Commonwealth

1650

14 Further reading

Print
General works

Jonathan Bate and Eric Rasmussen, eds. 'General Introduction' in *The RSC Shakespeare: The Complete Works* (Palgrave Macmillan, 2007). A useful starting point for studying Shakespeare and/or the Elizabethan and Jacobean contexts of the drama period.

Gordon Braden. *Renaissance Tragedy and the Senecan Tradition* (Yale University Press, 1987). Excellent on the importance of Seneca and stoicism to Jacobean tragedies of revenge.

N.S. Brooke. *Horrid Laughter in Jacobean Tragedy* (Barnes and Noble, 1979). Very good on the relationship between horror and humour in tragedy of this era.

Brian Gibbons. *Jacobean City Comedy*, 2nd edn (Methuen, 1980). A useful overview of the genre and especially helpful on Jonson's *Volpone*.

Stephen Greenblatt. *Renaissance Self-fashioning: From More to Shakespeare* (University of Chicago Press, 1980). A useful classic, for criticism and the contexts of the earlier Elizabethan plays of Marlowe and Jonson.

Stevie Simkin. *Marlowe: The Plays* (Palgrave Macmillan, 2001). A useful companion to studies on Marlowe's plays in their contexts.

Emma Smith and Garrett A. Sullivan Jr, eds. *The Cambridge Companion to English Renaissance Tragedy* (Cambridge University Press, 2010). A scholarly approach to the context of genre (in Part 1), approached through themes in tragedy. It has some useful and challenging essays in Part 2, on the plays you study by Kyd, Marlowe, Middleton, Webster and Ford.

The introduction in editions of the plays

The New Cambridge Shakespeare Series provides in-depth and scholarly introductions on the text and its contexts for each of his plays.

The introductions below are recommended for studying Elizabethan and Jacobean drama texts by Jonson, Marlowe, Middleton, Webster and Ford in context:

John O'Connor, ed. *Doctor Faustus* A-text (Longman Pearson, 2003). The thorough and clear guidance on the text and its contexts is excellent, especially in the section on contexts on pages 116–191.

R.A. Foakes, ed. Introduction. *The Revenger's Tragedy* (Manchester University Press, Revels Student Editions, 1996).

The editor's Introduction to the Methuen drama, New Mermaids series is particularly helpful for your study in these editions of the plays:

Brian Gibbons in *The Revenger's Tragedy*, 1991, and in *The Duchess of Malfi*, 2001.

Andrew Gurr in *The Spanish Tragedy*, 1989.

Christina Luckyj in *The White Devil*, 2003.

Robert N. Watson in *Volpone*, 2003.

Martin Wiggins in *Edward the Second*, 1997, and in *'Tis Pity She's a Whore*, 2003.

Online
On the literary, social and political contexts of the period

Here are some suggestions but you can also search the internet for these topics to find podcasts, lectures and other learning resources that will help you in your studies.

http://shakespearean.org.uk: search for a lecture by a teacher on Elizabethan and Jacobean theatre contexts.

http://anarchon.tripod.com: search for theatre history on the Ancient Greeks for information on Greek contexts.

www.wwnorton.com/college/english/nael/welcome. htm: *The Norton Anthology of English Literature online* – on period contexts and available historical and literary contextual sources/resources, including extracts of a translation of Montaigne's essay 'Of Cannibals'.

http://faculty.history.wisc.edu/sommerville/367/367-04. htm: on the Divine Right of Kings.

www.theatredatabase.com: search for 16th-century theatre and *commedia dell'arte*.

In addition you could search for free podcasts of Oxford University lectures by Emma Smith in Elizabethan and Jacobean drama.

Theatres and actors

www.elizabethan-era.org.uk: useful for the Elizabethan and Jacobean theatre in general, especially information on Blackfriars Theatre and the shift to indoor theatre, maps and sites of Elizabethan theatres.

www.globe-theatre.org.uk: on acting styles at the Globe and the theatre itself.

www.theatredatabase.com: useful for information on the 16th and 17th centuries, including the appearance of women on the stage, 17th-century theatre closures and the condemnation of the Elizabethan theatre in the 16th century.

The playwrights

Jonson:	www.notablebiographies.com
Marlow:	www.the-tudors.org.uk
	www.marlowe-society.org
Middleton:	http://thomasmiddleton.org
Shakespeare:	www.william-shakespeare.info
	www.bl.uk/treasures/shakespeare/basics.html
	www.bardweb.net/plays/timeline.html
Webster:	www.johnwebster.galeon.com

Resources on the BBC

The BBC has plenty of resources for Shakespeare and all aspects of Elizabethan and Jacobean drama, so a search on its website will provide lots of useful and up-to-date information. Recent resources at the time of this publication included the following.

Radio 4 podcasts

- Neil MacGregor exploring the world of Shakespeare and his audience through 20 objects from that turbulent period.

- *In Our Time*, Radio 4, 'Culture: Elizabethan Revenge' with Melvyn Bragg. Guests: Jonathan Bate, Julie Sanders and Janet Clare. Informative overview and discussion with the finest scholars of the day.

Videos: *Shakespeare Unlocked, A Midsummer Night's Dream* and *Macbeth*. RSC actors and directors unlock these plays – a great resource for students and teachers, including at GCSE.

A three-part TV programme: *The King and the Playwright*. Professor James Shapiro on the relationship between James I's rule and Shakespeare's output at that time.

Glossary

A

anagnorisis   the moment the tragic hero realises that his flaw has partly caused the tragedy.

aside   a character speaks privately to the audience whilst other characters are on the stage.

audience sympathy   a response of care and understanding towards the dilemmas and fortunes of a character.

C

comic subplot/comic relief comic scenes in tragedy that provide funny, light relief from the tragic plot and can emphasise important themes.

contemporary   something happening within its own time. This can be in the past or the present. For example, Jacobean contemporary matters are those happening in that period. Today's contemporary issues are those happening now, even at this moment.

context   a range of factors affecting how texts are written, received and understood.

cue acting   a backstage prompt whispered the actor's lines before he had to perform them.

cue scripting   the actor only saw the lines for his own part.

D

dialogue   characters speak with each other.

dramatic irony   the audience or reader knows something about a character that the other characters do not know, which has significance in the plot.

dumb show   short, often serious, ritualised episode without speech. A dumb show presents, mimics or foreshadows significant developments to plot or themes.

E

epic   celebrates the feats of a hero, often legendary, in a similar style and structure to a long narrative poem.

G

genre   a specific type of text. In literature there are three: drama, poetry and prose.

groundling   someone too poor to buy a seat, who stood in the cramped open-air pit to watch the play.

H

hamartia   the fatal flaw (or mistake) of a tragic hero.

I

ideology   political, social and cultural beliefs and ideas.

intertextual   has two meanings: 1 a text responds to ideas, language or direct references adopted or adapted from an earlier text. 2 within his or her own text, a writer refers to another's work or textual innovations.

M

macro   the overview or 'big picture': these contexts are concerned with the world outside of the play.

melancholic   a thoughtful, introverted loner.

micro   the detailed view: these contexts arise from the literary and theatrical conventions within the text itself or from the individual circumstances of the writer.

monologue   a character makes a speech to other, listening characters.

P

pander   a Jacobean pimp.

pathetic fallacy   the use of weather and landscape to reflect or symbolise human emotions.

patriarchy   a political and social system of male inheritance and dominance, enshrined in law or/and culture across all social classes and family structures.

period   a particular time or era in history.

protagonist   the principal character in the play.

Puritan
Puritan   a member of the movement (Puritanism) who believed in a basic, restrained lifestyle, both public and private, in terms of religious ceremony, entertainment, dress and behaviour.

R

reception   how we experience, understand and receive ideas, products and events.

revenge tragedy   focuses on the motive, planning and execution of death by revenge – usually several deaths.

S

satire   ironic comedy used to mock and judge people, groups or organisations and their vices – for example vulgar greed.

soliloquy   a character speaks privately to the audience when alone on the stage.

stoic(ism)   the Ancient Roman philosophy of enduring pain and suffering with quiet calm and dignity.

U

unsympathetic   the reaction by the audience when they do not understand the motives and behaviour of a character.

Index

A

actors and acting 78–85
amphitheatres 37, 98, 100
anagnorisis 35
Aristotle 34
asides 83

B

biographical contexts 18–20
boy players 79

C

Caroline era 24, 108
chaos 59
characters 64–77
city comedies 43, 88
classical influences 26–7, 46, 88
clowns 70–1
comedy 41–3, 54, 67
comic relief 23, 33
Commedia dell'arte 106
context 4, 6–8
culture 11–13, 24–30

D

death 54–6, 60
deception 82
disguise and concealment 60–1
Doctor Faustus 15–16, 28, 70
dramatic irony 82
dramatic techniques 80–3
dumb shows 23, 81

E

Elizabethan era 21–2, 107
England, plays set in 87–8
English Renaissance 14, 21, 24–30
exotica 30, 91–2

F

Ford, John 19, 39

G

genres 4, 14–15, 33–43, 46
Greek influences 26–7, 34–7

H

hamartia 34–5
Hamlet 28, 39, 45–6, 79–80

heroes 34–6, 68, 69
historical context 10–11, 21–30, 107–8
history plays 40–1, 54
honour 57
horrid laughter 33
humanism 27–8

I

interpretation 17–18
intertextuality 19–20, 47–8
Italy, use as setting 90–1

J

Jacobean era 22–4, 108
Jonson, Ben 19, 43, 70
journeys 89
justice 22, 56

K

Kyd, Thomas 20, 22, 104–5

L

law and punishment 56–7
literary contexts 12, 14–17, 33–43
love 60–1, 74

M

macro contexts 9, 10–13, 66
madness 59, 71
malcontents 69–70
Marlowe, Christopher 19, 22, 36
Master of Revels 103
micro contexts 9
Middleton, Thomas 19, 20
monologues 83
motifs 15–17
murder 55

N

natural settings 89

O

order and disorder 58–9
overacting 79

P

pastoral comedies 43
play within the play 81
playhouses 78, 98, 100–1

plots 45–52
political context 10–11, 21–4, 107–8
power 11, 58, 67, 72–3
Protestantism 24, 25–6

R

reception 7, 9, 17–18, 34
religious characters 69
Renaissance 14, 24–30
revenge tragedy 14, 22, 38–9, 55–6, 104
The Revenger's Tragedy 20, 39, 47
Roman influences 26, 37–8
rulers 58, 66–8

S

Seneca (Roman philosopher) 38
servants 73
settings 86–95
sex and lust 60
Shakespeare, William 19, 36, 43, 70, 88
social class 10–11, 73–4
soliloquies 83
sources, use of 45–6
The Spanish Tragedy 22, 31–2, 104–5
stock characters 42
stoicism 38
subgenres 14–15, 36, 40–1, 42–3
supernatural figures 74–5

T

theatre companies 101–3
theatres 30, 78, 96–101
themes 53–63
tragedy 33, 34–40, 41, 55–6, 67, 104
tragi-comedy 43, 54–5, 67

V

villains 68–9

W

weather 89–90
Webster, John 19, 39, 74
women 58, 71–2, 79
working classes 73–4